# CHILDREN, FAMILIES AND COMMUNITIES

## Creating and Sustaining Integrated Services

**Education in an Urbanised Society**

*Series Editors: Gerald Grace, Meg Maguire and Ian Menter*

Education continues to face a range of problems, crises, issues and challenges. Often, although not exclusively, those experiencing the most severe problems are working within an urban context. Such schools face very particular challenges – high ethnic minority intake, pupil underachievement, problems of teacher recruitment and retention, social deprivation and other factors. Teachers themselves need to be prepared for classes with a rapid turnover of pupils, pupils from homeless and refugee families, and pupils with English as an additional language.

This series is intended to help education professionals and academics gain a broader understanding of the challenges faced. It examines the problems facing teachers and learners working in challenging and dif?cult circumstances, with a view to overcoming disadvantage in contemporary education in the UK and Ireland. It explores social and educational developments and provides educational practitioners, academics and policy makers with focused analyses of key issues facing schools in an urban society, examining the interaction between theory and practice. It offers insights into the linkage between education development and wider social, cultural and economic needs and thus contributes to the achievement of social justice in and through education.

*Current titles*

Mel Ainscow and Mel West: *Improving Urban Schools*

Pat Broadhead, Chrissy Meleady and Marco A. Delgado: *Children, Families and Communities: Creating and Sustaining Integrated Services*

Meg Maguire, Tim Woodridge and Simon Pratt-Adams: *The Urban Primary School*

Jill Rutter: *Refugee Children in the UK*

# CHILDREN, FAMILIES AND COMMUNITIES

## Creating and Sustaining Integrated Services

PAT BROADHEAD
CHRISSY MELEADY
MARCO A. DELGADO

 Open University Press

Open University Press
McGraw-Hill Education
McGraw-Hill House
Shoppenhangers Road
Maidenhead
Berkshire
England
SL6 2QL

email: enquiries@openup.co.uk
world wide web: www.openup.co.uk

and Two Penn Plaza, New York, NY 10121–2289, USA

First published 2008
Copyright © The Authors 2008

A catalogue record of this book is available from the British Library

ISBN–10 0335220932 (pb) 0335220940 (hb)
ISBN–13 9780335220939 (pb) 9780335220946 (hb)


Library of Congress Cataloguing-in-Publication Data
CIP data applied for

Typeset by YHT Ltd, London
Printed in the UK by Bell and Bain Ltd, Glasgow

The McGraw-Hill Companies

# CONTENTS

# SERIES EDITORS' PREFACE

With policies such as Sure Start and Every Child Matters sweeping across England and beyond, and with local authorities moving increasingly towards the provision of integrated children's services, this volume, *Children, Families and Communities*, could not be more significant. Throughout the UK and Europe there has been increasing recognition over recent years that public services need to be 'joined up'. Children, their parents and carers do not lead their lives in separate compartments, where education, health and social welfare are distinct needs. People's needs are complex and continuously changing and children's needs can change more rapidly than those of adults.

Running through this book is a gripping narrative that demonstrates with passion and commitment how it is possible to meet at least some of the challenges that face young people and their families in an economically depressed and rapidly changing community. But at the centre of the story are not the paid and qualified workers, skilful and hard working though they are. Rather it is the voices of members of the community themselves that come through so clearly in this story. We read of lives transformed through association with the Sheffield Children's Centre; we read of lives saved and lost – it really is that serious – and we read of the tensions that can occur when a social movement within a disadvantaged community really does develop a voice of its own and can come into conflict with the institutions that have responsibility for funding, resources and provision.

The story is not always a happy one, but it is one that demonstrates something of the possibilities of community action and development around provision that is formally classified as simply a children's centre. It is a story that will capture the imagination of those who seek to work in such settings, or who wish to bring about improvement and create opportunity in the most disadvantaged urban areas.

As the editors of this series, we could not have wished for a more appropriate text to tackle the questions of provision for families and for the youngest children in urban settings. We are grateful to Pat Broadhead, Marco Delgado and Chrissy Meleady for this account of the development of the centre. They have sought to provide an accurate account of a complicated sequence of events with authenticity and with deep respect for the integrity and rights of the other actors in this scene. Not only have they achieved this, but through their own reflection and analysis they have also enabled us to understand some of the social processes – including processes of conflict, conflict resolution, political negotiation and community integration – that have been at play throughout the development of the centre.

The book therefore works at many levels and we are sure will be of interest to students, activists, policy-makers and politicians. But most of all it is a book that will fire the imagination, that demonstrates the power of the human spirit, where there is goodwill and where there is a collective commitment to social justice.

*Ian Menter*
*on behalf of Gerald Grace and Meg Maguire*

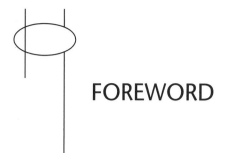

# FOREWORD

This book tells the story of how a small community project, beginning life in a church hall, has grown to become a multifaceted and international network of services for children and their families – yet in the process has lost neither its identity nor its soul. The process has not been easy – indeed it has been a struggle, as the Sheffield Children's Centre has had to confront a range of obstacles, from racist vandals to the vagaries of government funding, or lack of it. It is a story that is moving, affirmative, thought-provoking, troubling and, above all, inspiring.

Moving because the centre is a living example of how a service can work with an ethic of care, responding to new needs and cries for help from families living in its hinterland in Sheffield. Faced by these needs and cries for help, the centre's response has never been to pass by on the other side, to suggest that families try some other service, but to ask 'What can we do, how can we provide "culturally appropriate support"?' The centre has consistently shown a sustained and deep-seated sense of responsibility, without any conditions or calculation of return.

Read the family vignettes in Chapter 2 to see what I mean, as families recount how the centre has supported them through a range of harrowing problems: immigration, illness, terminal illness (of children and parents), death and bereavement, abuse and domestic violence, teenage pregnancy and drugs. Or turn to the vignettes in Chapter 3, which tell of how the centre has supported families in their struggles with various government agencies, advocating to get justice and entitlements even at the price of making the centre itself more vulnerable. Or read the accounts in Chapter 5 of the centre's work in Ethiopia, Jordan, Pakistan and Zimbabwe, in response to direct requests from local communities in those countries, 'an inevitable progression of principles in action'.

Affirmative because the centre shows that ideas that I have personally long harboured as theoretical and highly desirable possibilities can, in fact, be put into practice. Take the case of the workforce in early childhood services. I am not alone in believing that far more men are needed to work in these services; the present 2 per cent of male nursery workers sends a clear but mistaken signal that young children are 'women's work'. But the Sheffield Children's Centre is the only service I have ever come across that has aimed for, and achieved, a genuinely gender-mixed workforce, and by so doing shown that such diversity is possible.

And the reason? I suspect the answer lies in the centre's passionate belief and commitment to diversity. It is a place where 'diversity is the norm, not the exception', and this commitment can be seen in the many other dimensions of diversity represented in the workforce, and the centrality of diversity to every aspect of the centre's life, its policy, provision and practice.

It is also affirming because it shows how an early childhood institution can be a site for democratic political practice. As such the centre figured in a book I wrote with Gunilla Dahlberg, *Ethics and Politics in Early Childhood Education*:

> The Sheffield Children's Centre provides a vivid example of the political potential of preschools (and other institutions for children). In all aspects of their existence – organisation, workforce and practices – the Centre [has] shown how a preschool can become a site for democratic 'minor politics', in particular around questions of difference and injustice.
>
> (Dahlberg and Moss, 2005: 175)

The current book amply reaffirms this earlier assessment of the centre's significance; it is a rich study of the political role of an early childhood institution, as well as of how such an institution can practise democracy in its everyday work.

Thought-provoking because the book combines rich accounts of and by the centre's staff, children and families with some important theoretical reflections. The authors relate their story to theories of social and cultural capital, describing the centre as 'an architect' of such capital, 'working to confront a world that remains unequal for many of its inhabitants'. Following the work of the Spanish sociologist Manuel Castells, the authors also suggest that Sheffield Children's Centre can be read as a social movement and one that has moved from a resistance to a project identity: 'the work at Sheffield Children's Centre grew out of an ethic of resistance to cultural inappropriateness for vulnerable children and families; from this its project identity emerged and became influential'. In that journey from resistance to project identity, minority groups have moved from opposing established norms to gradually becoming innovative agents, shaping services to meet their needs and to be responsive to their lives.

The authors describe the centre as offering both a heartland of influence upon the wider community and a catalyst for change:

> As the *heartland*, in the early days, [the centre] gradually drew increasing numbers of individuals and groups into its landscape . . . As the *catalyst*, it began to reflect back to a range of service users a renewed and invigorated sense of their cultural identity by becoming increasingly effective

at understanding, encompassing and promoting diversity through its services.

Thought-provoking, too, because the centre has operated as a co-operative, a mode of organisation uncommon for this type of service in England (though more common in some other countries, such as Italy). At a time when government policy highlights the importance of leadership in children's services, it is unusual and provoking to be confronted by a model of democratic control, especially in such a complex and multifaceted institution. Is Sheffield in this respect just a one-off, the exception that proves the rule? Or could the co-operative have a larger role to play in children's services, especially if greater prominence were to be given to democracy as a value?

Troubling because, despite its innovative qualities, despite its responsiveness, not least its ability to draw in the widest range of families (including those sometimes referred to by government as 'hard to reach'), despite its commitment to diversity and participation, despite its unique body of knowledge and experience, the centre has not had an easy relationship with the powers that be. Funding has been a perennial and debilitating problem; recognition as an Early Excellence Centre has not been followed by Children's Centre status; and relationships with the local authority, Sheffield City Council, have at times been fraught rather than supportive.

Is this exceptional, a unique catalogue of unfortunate incidents? Or does this story say something worrying about how government in England finds it difficult to value and support non-profit providers that are innovative and challenging, committed to fighting for their families and communities, that don't neatly fit the boxes, that take diversity and participation seriously? Is it 'in spite of' or 'because of'? This book can, and should, be treated as a sustained case study that will repay close examination by politicians, policy-makers and anyone else interested in public services, community regeneration and the revival of democracy.

And, finally, it is inspiring, for the Sheffield Children's Centre is a reason to be hopeful. In the words of Gilles Deleuze, it gives cause 'to believe in the world' again. It is an example of utopian thinking made utopian action – 'the exploration by imagination of new modes of human possibility' (Santos, 1995: 481) – linked to an exploration in practice of these modes of possibility. It is an example not of best practice, but of utopian practice rooted in collective decisions about what is the right thing to do. It is an example of the democratisation of education and other services for children and families. It is an example of deep respect for diversity and justice. It is an example of a form of globalisation in which local actions that share values connect up to form networks of mutual support and exchange.

Are more Sheffield Children's Centres needed? Not if that means 'rolling out' some national programme of identikit Sheffields, working to standardised guidelines. Sheffield Children's Centre is too much the product of time and place to be replicated; it is a provocation not a blueprint. But, yes, I would say if it means giving recognition and support to other community groups – other local social movements – who want to put their own utopian thought into action, to find and act on their own critical questions.

Some years ago, I visited an Italian city – not Reggio Emilia – that had developed over many years a wonderful network of early childhood centres. The director of these services described that community's work in developing this network as a 'local cultural project of childhood'. That term could, I think, apply to Sheffield Children's Centre, for in both cases there has been a recognition of public responsibility to local children as valued citizens of their community, and a commitment, sustained over time, to giving culturally appropriate meaning to that responsibility.

*Peter Moss*

# A NOTE ON THE AUTHORS

The three authors of this book have been involved with the centre in various capacities and for differing periods of time. It will be helpful to readers to know something of this involvement.

**Chrissy Meleady MBE** was a founder member of Sheffield Children's Centre and of the St Mary's Programme that preceded the centre. Chrissy was awarded the MBE for working with children, families and communities in Britain and overseas. She was for a long period both Head of Centre and Chair of the Management Committee of the centre, which comprises service users – adults, children and young people – workers, paid and unpaid and members of the local community. Chrissy has been an advocate for the centre since its inception, has organised and presented at conferences and parliamentary committees and has written about the work of the centre in numerous publications. The centre hosts many visits from national and international delegates. Chrissy is currently Chief Executive of Early Years Equality and was previously Chief Executive of Sheffield Racial Equality Council and South Yorkshire Race Discrimination Service. She has also been a Human Rights Commissioner. Chrissy is currently a service user at the centre, which two of her children continue to attend.

**Pat Broadhead** is Professor of Playful Learning at Leeds Metropolitan University. Her earliest links with the centre came when she was a member of the Sheffield Childcare Campaign. This group was approached by the then St Mary's Community Programme to support its intention to retain local services as the community programmes were closed. Later, Pat offered curriculum development activities to the workers at the centre and supported the development of some of its policy documents and practices. When the Centre was designated an Early Excellence Centre, Pat was invited to become the external evaluator over a three-year period, a time during which some of the data that form the basis for this book were gathered. Much of these data also informed reports presented in relation to evaluation activities within the

Early Excellence Centre programme, documents now in the public domain. Pat has continued supporting the centre in its planned developments for an expanded service, and has been present at many of its meetings with local authority representatives around this aspect. She and Chrissy Meleady have published jointly and presented at conferences on the work of the centre.

Prior to registering for his PhD at the University of York, **Marco Delgado** had worked with non-governmental organisations (NGOs) and within the Mexican Government to improve services for children in his home country. Introduced to the centre by Pat Broadhead, Marco located a substantial part of his PhD research in Sheffield Children's Centre and spent 18 months in this fieldwork. The doctorate was awarded in 2006 and provides a substantial part of the theoretical framework for this book. As an overseas student at the centre, Marco was able to connect in many ways with the experiences of some ethnic-minority service users in relation to dealing with cultural adaptation in a new context, and in reflecting on the importance of identity and belonging in culturally unfamiliar contexts. Marco came to see connections between the work of the centre and the aspirations and intentions of similar initiatives he had encountered in his work in Mexico, as well as in relation to other Latin American countries. Some of these perspectives are used in this book. Marco has returned to Mexico and is currently working for an NGO whose name translates as 'Towards a Democratic Society' (ACUDE in Spanish). This organization undertakes educational research, mainly on preschool education. It focuses its efforts in promoting social involvement, transparency and participative evaluation. Within its research, ACUDE collaborates with other national and international NGOs, with government and with scholars to influence policy development in Mexico.

With such extensive links to the centre between them, the authors cannot claim to be wholly impartial observers in its work and development, and we would not wish to claim this. We doubt this book could be written by anyone who has not been connected to the day-to-day work of the centre in some capacity; one has to be an insider to some extent to describe this work in convincing detail, and to be trusted by workers and service users in gathering the data.

The extent of our individual connections to the centre does vary in terms of time and contributions to its development. Chrissy's connection is the most substantial among the authors, being a founder member of the centre. Marco's association is, in terms of time spent associated with the centre, the least extensive, although during his period of data collection, he did undertake a deep immersion in the day-to-day work of the centre. He also shared the emerging findings with workers and parents. It was perhaps his more distanced stance, alongside the requirements of his thesis, that enabled him to create such a convincing theoretical framework. Marco was able to theorise that which Chrissy and, to a lesser extent, Pat, were more substantially immersed within.

Given Pat's 'halfway-house' connections to the centre, and Marco's return to Mexico on successful completion of the thesis, it seemed sensible for Pat to take the lead author role on the developing chapters. She was able to draw on Marco's thesis for substantial contribution and to liaise closely with Chrissy as the chapters emerged to check the accuracy of the content and to ensure that the essence of the chapters truly reflected the ethos of the centre. Chrissy and Marco also edited the emerging chapters and each of us sought to ensure that our partiality and subjectivity was overruled by a discerning use of the data available and by the desire to communicate the theoretical framework in an accessible and enlightening way. Workers at the centre have also seen, discussed, and helped to develop these chapters.

# ACKNOWLEDGEMENTS

Our thanks go to the workers and service users – the children, young people and adults – who *are* Sheffield Children's Centre. We hope you feel we have captured the essence of the centre and done justice to your work, your relationships, and your aspirations for social change and equity in a still unequal society.

Our combined thanks go also to Professor Peter Moss for writing the Foreword to this book with his usual grace and insight, both of the centre and in terms of his national and international understanding of service development. Peter has had a long-standing association over many years with and remains a good friend to the Sheffield Children's Centre.

Our thanks go also to Ian Menter as responding series editor for his insightful and always helpful and encouraging comments and feedback.

# INTRODUCTION

This book describes the work of Sheffield Children's Centre. The centre is a community co-operative that has operated for over 20 years in an inner-city setting of economic disadvantage. It has been developing and offering services to children and families in the local community and beyond, long before the more recent designation of 'Children's Centres' within government policy.

A visitor arriving at Sheffield Children's Centre would find themselves walking along a short path, with a busy road behind them and leading to a high fence. On the left they would see an enclosed outdoor grassed play area with large, sturdily constructed climbing frames, swings and so on – a typical outdoor play space but overlooking the busy road. On the right, the visitor would see a small parking area. The visitor would arrive at a gate with an intercom to admit entrance to the main area of the centre.

As the visitor proceeded through the gate, she would arrive into a good-sized outdoor play space. She would see the main building directly opposite: a long, rectangular, clearly old, one-storey prefabricated building with a pitched roof. To the left is a covered outdoor area set against the outer wall, and a storage area for outdoor toys. To the right is a separate prefabricated building, also one storey. This smaller building has two main rooms, quite large, and is used for the out-of-school centre, for training sessions and for meetings.

The main building is across the rectangular playground. The visitor would enter a reception area. To the right of this area is a kitchen where meals are prepared and there is a small room used for changing babies' nappies. This smaller room is off one of the three main bases in this main area. This base provides for babies and young toddlers. There are also storage areas adjoining the baby room, and a room with cots to allow sleep and rest for the babies and toddlers. If the visitor goes to the left of reception she will proceed down a narrow corridor. Off to the left of this corridor are a rest room and a separate adult toilet and cloakroom area. To the right are the main office, with three desks/working spaces, and a separate work room with a photocopier, tables and chairs, resources and so on.

The visitor would pass through another door and then enter the two further bases. One provides for the older toddlers, aged from 2 to 3, and one is the early education setting for 3 and 4 year olds. There is also a large area used for quiet activities and for sleep and rest. The children's toilets are in this area. At the back of the centre is a large, publicly accessible grassed area that the centre children also use on occasion.

The centre is open from 8 am until 6 pm every day except public holidays. The following extract from Delgado's work (2006: 210) gives a brief description of the inside:

> The interiors are decorated with images of children of different races, with adults, women and men of different ages playing and interacting with children in different ethnic and European dress. From the entrance, the centre is multi-lingual, with notices in different languages and alphabets. Handmade toys also reflect the cultural diversity of the centre. Diversity is also found in notices for adults and children which are located at different heights on the walls. This is an acknowledgement of the different heights of children and adults and also of the centre's wheelchair users. The value of cultural diversity and the promotion of meaningful relationships between children and staff of both genders are integral to centre policy.

Although the buildings are old, they are well maintained but as Maggie, a long-standing worker at the centre, remarked: 'The building is an old Quonset hut, temporarily built in 1943, and it's still here. We've replaced the roofs and the internal structure, which cost us over a quarter of a million, but it's now deteriorating.'

As the story of Sheffield Children's Centre unfolds over the forthcoming chapters, something will be seen of the lives and aspirations of those who work within and who use these spaces: the children, the young people and the adults. But the centre is not an island, it is connected to a wider community in many ways and this will also become apparent as the story unfolds as an integral part of the centre's story, its activities, its difficulties and its successes.

This is not only a story of Sheffield Children's Centre, it is also an attempt to illustrate how this exploration of the centre contributes to a better understanding of the socio-cultural and socio-political contexts within which this country's expanding services for children and families are located. We could not tell this story without some reference to government policy, particularly since 1997 and the return of the Labour government, but this is not the main thrust of the book by any means. We hope this book will help the reader not only to understand the centre and its work but also to see its impact not only as a provider of services but also as an architect of social and cultural capital working to confront a world that remains unequal for many of its inhabitants. Brunsden and May (2002) discuss the extent to which the Blair government espoused non-statutory welfare, and encompassed voluntary and community organisations and commercial service providers to achieve this. This is by no means a key theme for the book and we will not engage with their critique of Labour policy. However, their argument gives an indication of the wider context of political change, which has been paralleling the centre's growth in more recent years. Brunsden and May draw on the work of Putnam, (1993) and Giddens (1998) to suggest that New Labour's proposals were powered by a fundamental anxiety over the state of civil society. There was a perceived need to rebuild social capital as a prerequisite for economic regeneration in deprived areas and for the reconstruction of responsible citizenship. Both the Sheffield Children's Centre and the state may be architects of social capital in their own ways, and in this book we make explicit the underpinning principles for action at Sheffield Children's Centre as they work for equity and parity.

Chapter 1 depicts the evolution of the centre from a community programme in purpose-built spaces in a church hall. This first phase of its development was established under a Conservative government. Through relocation, the centre entered its second phase of development to become a multifaceted community provider with a clear and well-expanded identity, located in then adequate but gradually deteriorating buildings. The chapter illustrates the extent of the centre's developing work through a focus on the wide range of types of worker associated with the centre, and offers some detailed descriptions, in their own words, of their work within and association with the centre. The workforce is deliberately multicultural and multiethnic, with a recruitment policy of 50 per cent men. Chapter 1 introduces two key terms that run throughout the book, describing the centre as a *heartland* of influence upon the wider community and, resulting from this, as a *catalyst for change* via its services and fundamental tenets of practice. The chapter describes the gradual emergence of a *project identity* for the Sheffield Children's Centre and explains how this identity reflects the desire of ordinary people to influence social change based on local demands. The centre began because local people expressed concerns about the cultural inappropriateness of mainstream provision close by, and it grew because its aim was to reflect diversity in all its practices. This aspiration has been both its strength and its greatest challenge, and locates the centre, as described by Dahlberg and Moss (2005: 171), as a 'site for democratic practice and minor politics'.

Chapter 2 provides detail on the centre's work with families, recognising the child's cultural heritage within the family and the community as a starting point for service development and integrity. The heartland is described in terms of the people who use the centre, and the services they access and that are created in response to expressed need by community members; expressed need is illustrated as an integral part of service development. The catalyst for change arises from the interface between the community and the services – but only because the centre puts the promotion of diversity at the heart of the heartland. In this chapter, we see the centre's engagement with children's rights and examine a series of family vignettes where respondents detail the difficulties and distresses of their own lives and the centre's work to support them at these difficult times. As they move on from their difficulties, many of them subsequently bring skills and contributions to the centre's work; this reciprocity becomes an outcome from principles and practice. Chapter 2 begins to challenge the construct of community members being 'hard to reach' – a well-used term in recent government policy – by illustrating the centre's successes and the factors that underpin them. The chapter also details the centre's progression to being designated an Early Excellence Centre within emerging Labour policy.

Sheffield Children's Centre is a community-based provision run on co-operative lines, an independent provider that must secure funding to remain viable. Chapter 3 describes what this means for the centre and examines the implications for leadership and visioning in the centre. Building on some strands evident in the preceding chapters, Chapter 3 begins to examine what the implications might be in terms of relationships with the local authority. Sheffield Children's Centre was one of a very small number of Early Excellence Centres that did not sit within a local authority jurisdiction and this has undoubtedly created some difficulties for it for a range of reasons. In pursuing a social justice agenda for children and community members, centre workers have often advocated on their behalf and against the local authority; some of this advocacy work is described here, and illustrative commentary seeks to unpack the wider implications. The chapter ends with perspectives from local authority representatives and others who sit 'outside' the centre but know of its work. This section considers how differing starting points for practice can create fundamentally different perspectives on what constitutes good practice in provision for young children. As Moss and Pence (1994) have illustrated, different stakeholders may hold different views on what constitutes quality and good practice.

Chapter 4 focuses on the promotion of diversity and what this really means; it uses the metaphor of diversity as a 'diamond with many facets' to show the extent of the 'cutting and polishing' needed to put policy into practice if respect for diversity is to underpin all practices. The chapter also illustrates the difficulties of being a cutting-edge provider with diversity at its heart, when other community members might come to resent the growing identity and impact of a service for children and families; this brings unwelcome attention for the centre. Chapter 4 looks at men in childcare, and how centre policy has been received and developed within the centre and beyond. It looks at intergenerational care to illustrate more of the centre's work 'from cradle to grave'. It describes the emergence and development of the Female Genital Mutilation Group, illustrative of the substantial trust that some of the most marginalised community members have come to have in the centre. The chapter discusses the principles underpinning the Fit Kids Club and talks also about mental health support for adults and for children. It also focuses on children's learning and examines the broad way in which the curriculum is defined at the centre, incorporating but going beyond existing curriculum guidelines. Chapter 4 illustrates the centre's belief that the child's cultural heritage and personal experiences are the starting points for his or her curricular experiences and not an addition, afterthought or optional extra.

Chapter 5 introduces the international work of the centre that has developed over the years. This is presented not as additional activity but as an inevitable progression of principles in action. In developing the discussion around *project identity*, which has so far comprised the constructs of *heartland* and *catalyst for change*, this chapter introduces the relevance of *social and cultural capital* to a conceptual understanding of how the centre works and develops. The chapter describes examples of international work in Ethiopia, Jordan, Pakistan, Zimbabwe and Somalia. It describes work linked with Ireland, and with the Catholic Church and related organisations. It concludes with a reiteration of the underpinning principles of practice informing both national and international service provision.

The final chapter has two sections. First, it details the more recent links with the local authority set within the substantial policy developments and funding streams there have been in the area of provision for children and families since 1997. Expanding government policy and local authority interpretation of that policy swirl around the centre's work and visioning, and we interconnect these aspects in this first section. It describes the steps the centre has taken to progress as the new century began, seeking to build on its Early Excellence Centre status and to enter a third phase of development with new buildings and an expanded site to house the extensive and always developing services.

The second part of Chapter 6, the conclusion to the book, draws together the conceptual framework for describing and understanding the centre's work in its partnerships with and the impact upon the local community and beyond. It asks what the implications are for the development of mainstream services from this long-standing community-based initiative; it also asks whether there are fundamental responsibilities for local and national governments to nurture cutting-edge services that develop from starting points and that are driven by principles of practice that are different from their own.

*All the names used in the book are pseudonyms, except those of the authors.*

# THE EVOLUTION OF SHEFFIELD CHILDREN'S CENTRE: DEVELOPING A PROJECT IDENTITY

The rewards are immense. In a centre of this kind you can't remain in a gap; our lines find each other and our work inevitably overlaps because of the nature of the children's and the families' needs. It is a sense of community and that none of us is alone. Often people will help you to help others and it's this gentleness which is most rewarding for me and to see the fight going back into people who have been stamped on.

(Maggie, centre founder member)

The statistics for the year 2000, for the Sharrow ward in which the Sheffield Children's Centre is located, illustrate the demographics of the local community at the time when the above reflection on the centre and its work was offered by Maggie:

- 62 per cent of birth–4 year olds were living in low-income families
- 41 per cent of birth–4 year olds were living in out-of-work families
- the average of 5–15 year olds in either out-of-work or in-work low-income families was higher in the ward than in either the county or national averages
- 40 per cent of birth–15 year olds were living in out-of-work families.

In setting Maggie's reflection alongside these statistics, we can see that the local population being served by the centre was one in which many, although by no means all, of its members were well acquainted with poverty.

The consequences of poverty on the quality of life and on child development are well documented; the economic position of the family is strongly affected by both the present and future welfare of the children (Gregg *et al.*, 1999). The intergenerational effects of poverty are long-standing, affecting the cognitive development of both parents and children and the cross-generational potential for future income generation. Millar and Ridge (2002: 87) document the 'promise to end child poverty' of the present government as emerging in 1999 in a speech by Blair (Blair, 1999: 7). The 1980s and 1990s had seen a threefold increase in the numbers of children living in poverty during the period of the Conservative government. The work of Rahman *et al.* (2000) was influential; their report built on a series of reports from the New Policy Institute, beginning with Howarth and Kenway (1998). Rahman *et al.* (2000) had shown that, as of 1998/99, there had been no reduction in the numbers of children living in poverty and there were four and a half million children in households with below half average income after housing costs were removed – one of the poorest records on child poverty in the developed world (Bradbury and Jantti, 1999). This trend was alarming and would substantially influence emerging government policy under New Labour, leading in due course to the Green Paper *Every Child Matters* (DfES, 2003) and the Children Act 2004.

Labour policy has aimed to lift children out of poverty. A key strand of this policy has been childcare, the means by which parents and carers might return to paid employment and/or training and further education en route to paid employment. The ten-year strategy for childcare (HM Treasury, 2004) states in paragraph 1.1:

> Early childhood is a time of vital importance in children's development. It is widely known that the quality of care that children receive in their early years makes a real difference to their development and later outcomes. Today's parents face considerable challenges balancing their work and family commitments. The demands of work in an increasingly competitive world economy and the need to ensure that all children have a good start in life mean that families can find it ever harder to strike the right work–life balance for them and their children. The way that Government responds to these challenges affects families' quality of life and the country's economic prosperity.

Here, quite clearly, the government emphasis is substantially upon economic prosperity for the country overall, echoing long-standing exhortations to become the 'economic tigers' of the future. This is an international preoccupation of many governments as globalisation equates with effective competition in an increasingly competitive global marketplace. The key challenge, however, is to keep the lives of the poor and oppressed in sight, simultaneously.

Government initiatives aim to improve levels of prosperity for all community members. This may not, however, be enough for the already disenfranchised, for those who, for example, are growing up in communities where adults exist both beyond the economic mainstream and outside the prevailing cultures of existing childcare services – what the Sure Start programme, through emerging government policy, termed the 'hard to reach' – a construct this book will challenge. It is not being suggested at this point that Sheffield Children's Centre provides for and responds only to the disenfranchised, but by studying its work and practice we see the extent of its success in reaching, acknowledging and celebrating diverse cultures, lifestyles and life choices, and for reaching those who, for whatever reason, locate themselves or find themselves located out of mainstream services. We begin to comprehend something of the centre's record of achievement in building trust and then, in reaching and assisting the disenfranchised members of its local community and beyond. We see also how its personal philosophies and experiences underpin its conceptual space and practices to become both the *catalyst for change* within its services and also a *heartland* of influence upon the wider community. The Introduction drew attention to the centrality of these terms in relation to the work of the centre, its aspirations and impact. As the book progresses, we aim to defend them as central constructs for underpinning integrated services where social exclusion prevails because of poverty, race, ethnicity, religion, sexuality and disability. Freire's work (1970, 1972, 1973, 1987, 1999) has addressed government responsibility to those living in exclusion. He writes of the importance of the voice of opposition and the implications for service development, maintaining that the voice of opposition could become the mainstream (Delgado, 2006). The voice of the oppressed must be heard in order to establish successful norms (Willis, 1999). In this chapter, we begin to examine how those voices are heard and responded to at Sheffield Children's Centre.

We will see how the children and families using the centre have confronted the difficulties that poverty brings. At the same time, we will try to convey the essence of the opening quote from Maggie and will aim to document a perceived strength at work in Sheffield Children's Centre; a strength that arises from a sense of unity, feelings of connectedness and a renaissance of self-belief. The centre's goal is not to return parents to work or to training; perhaps it does not have an equivalent 'direct goal', but it certainly aims to support parents and carers in making the right choices for themselves and their children, often in the face of considerable adversity. This links with the need for parents and carers to lift themselves and their families out of poverty. In helping families to achieve this, the centre's workers celebrate the 'return of fight' – the return of self-belief and self-determination as indicators of personal progress and ambition for the family and as an individual need within a supportive community. The difference perhaps is between the driving desire of government for a sound economy and a driving belief within the centre in the rights of the individual to be able to make choices about how they and their family will live their lives, within the broader context of community and society.

This first chapter considers how the spirit of the centre has emerged and grown over time; what has been the driving force for its growth, and where and to what extent this might put the centre in conflict with the bureaucracy of the mainstream. By identifying and reflecting on the roots of the centre, we aim to illustrate and then conceptualise its growth, into a time and place – the new millennium – where its well-established and wide-ranging services for children, family and community were, through the Early Excellence Centre initiative, typified as the blueprint for practice on a national scale. What we also aim to do, however, is illustrate how the centre's services are underpinned by some significantly different values and beliefs than those that came to underpin government policy in the roll-out of the national programme of Children's Centres.

## Starting out at Sheffield Children's Centre

Towards the end of the 1970s, and under a Labour government, some of the founder workers of Sheffield Children's Centre were offering a community programme that included childcare services for local people in a suite of rooms in a community centre/church hall situated about half a mile from where the current centre is situated. This provision was known as St Mary's Children's Centre. The programme offered return-to-work opportunities for the unemployed, and childcare services; in addition, it offered opportunities for local people to gain experiences and qualifications within the childcare sector from their work within the community programme. Some of the now long-standing workers at Sheffield Children's Centre began in this way, able to bring their own children with them while they were at work.

In 1989, the Conservative government withdrew the funding for the national community programme initiative. At the same time, it passed the Children Act 1989 (HMSO, 1989), the first major legislation to focus on children and which required that local authorities take responsibility for making provision for children 'in need'. Local authorities were beginning to take on the responsibilities that local communities had fulfilled within the community programme initiative.

The St Mary's Community Programme workers might have done what many others did at this point and closed their community services with considerable sadness. However, they believed that there was a need for such a service within the community. The only other service was offered by a local nursery school. A number of parents using the community programme had withdrawn their children from the local nursery school because they reported that they did not feel it offered appropriate experiences to their children from black or minority ethnic communities. There was a view that the local authority service was 'stigmatising and was unwilling to engage with parents about the need to change' (Franklin, 1999: 105). Seeing the imminence of closure, workers from the St Mary's Community Programme began their fight for continuity of provision within the local community and, in this, they worked alongside local parents and carers.

As far as the national policy agenda was concerned, childcare was not perceived by the Conservative government as a key policy driver, indeed as any kind of policy driver (Daniel and Ivatts, 1998). This would not change throughout the Tories' term and it might be argued that they were only prompted to a focus upon childcare by premonitions of loss of office. In 1996, they finally produced a consultation document on childcare (DfEE, 1996), which opens with the words, 'Responsibility for arranging care for children rests with parents and rightly so' (para. 1) and, a little later, 'It is Government policy that responsibility for childcare, including paying for it, rests with parents, not the State' (para. 6). Sensing the childcare desert that was emerging with the Tory return to office, the workers in St Mary's CP decided that if anything was to be done they were going to have to do it themselves.

Working with local parents, and taking advice from a range of sources, a decision was made to establish a service within the context of a community co-operative. In 1988 the Articles of Association were established for the newly emerging service. These outlined the collective practices that now underpin and direct the centre's management and delivery service. These practices are reviewed annually by the management committee. This committee comprised then and continues to include paid and unpaid workers, and service users including adults and children. The constitution is based on the practice of collectivity, underpinned by egalitarian principles. In due course, the centre achieved charitable status and became a company limited by guarantee.

However, at this point in time (1989), the paid and unpaid workers were continuing to offer the service in the rooms in the community centre/church hall. With the advent of the Children Act 1989, this was no longer suitable, as Jenny, a worker from the early days of the community programme, reflects:

> It was about five of us involved at this stage and the 1989 Children's Act came and asked for many requirements. So we found ourselves in a position where we had a building that couldn't accommodate the children, didn't fulfil the regulations and we couldn't build a fire stair for the children. So, we found this place and had to generate over quarter of a million pounds to move in here and we needed more staff.

'This place', to which Jenny refers, was a pair of prefabricated buildings with outbuildings and outdoor play space, as described in the Introduction. The buildings were intended for temporary use as a primary school when erected following bomb strikes in the city. They were then used as a depot for the Council's Works Department and, as the cost of maintaining the building increased, the Council relocated the depot and the buildings became vacant. The site stands about half a mile from the original location, the church hall, thus continuing to serve the same local community as previously.

Recognising the need to extend their expertise and knowledge, Jenny continued to reflect on her past experiences, on beginning to take greater responsibility for personnel, developing her appraisal skills and drawing on her own background as an accountant to take responsibility for the finances of the centre. While these skills have developed over time, in the early days the financial burdens were considerable:

> Generating the money has been difficult over all these years. There's been times in the office when we wanted to cry 'cos we needed £500 at the end of the week to pay the five of us, now it's more like £5000 at the end of the week. We have the insurance, tax and so forth . . . some people work here for nothing even if they have to find part-time jobs elsewhere.

So the service moved to buildings that needed refurbishment and that were not purpose-built for children, although they did offer access to good-sized spaces both indoors and outdoors. The staffing levels were quite low but sufficient for the then current activities. However, it was generally recognised that the service would need to expand in order to remain viable. Increasing numbers of local people were presenting themselves to the centre in search of support. Staff were prepared to work for low wages and to take on the additional financial challenges associated with the expansion of their work. They held a firm and shared belief that they would make it work because it was what the community needed, and it was also what the workers believed in and wanted to offer; many of the workers lived locally. They adopted the name Sheffield Children's Centre and began to establish the new service in close conjunction with their service users, both adults and children.

In the early days, the workers and parents agreed that they wanted a non-hierarchical organisation where service users (adults, young people and children) and service providers shared common ground and held equal status. Co-operatives had been in existence for at least 160 years by this point. They are equitable businesses with a social purpose, democratically owned and controlled by their members. There are nearly three-quarters of a million co-operatives worldwide, providing jobs for over 100 million people – more than are employed in all the multinational corporations throughout the world (Co-operative Action, undated). All businesses need long-term finance for their growth, development and sustainability. In the case of co-operatives the business itself is the source of its finance, with profits being reinvested in the business. This was the principle that was to secure the staffing, resources and training opportunities for the Sheffield Children's Centre.

It is recognised that childcare was probably one of the few services that could, at this point in time, actually flourish under a co-operative principle. Childcare is a mixed-provision service – that is, a service provided by a mix of public-sector, private-sector and voluntary-sector providers. Funding for childcare services has, for a long time in this country, come from a mixed economy of public subsidy, voluntary activity and direct private expenditure. Until the subsequent changes in government policy that would be forthcoming from the late 1980s, the opportunities for co-operative social enterprise to play a part in public service delivery had been limited (Reed and Stanley, 2005). Sheffield Children's Centre is recognised by Reed and Stanley as one of a small number of well-established childcare co-operatives, one that emerged at a time of policy shift in this arena and one that took increasing advantage of the co-operative philosophy for manifesting its shared beliefs in relation to supporting the needs of children, young people and families.

## Choosing to work at Sheffield Children's Centre

We now turn to reflections from a wide range of workers at Sheffield Children's Centre. These were gathered through face-to-face interviews during 2000 as part of the evaluation of the centre as an Early Excellence Centre. The interviews were transcribed and all transcriptions returned to respondents for amendments or deletion as they wished. Becoming an Early Excellence Centre is detailed further in Chapter 2, where we also begin to examine the emerging relationship between the Sheffield Children's Centre, working as a co-operative, and the local authority.

These extracts illustrate the wide range of workers now engaged within the centre as its work has grown over the years. Some have a daily association while others engage occasionally but regularly. Some are paid and some work in a voluntary capacity. Some are centre-based and others connect with the centre's work from a distance. Each of these individuals brings their skills and expertise to complement those of their colleagues and to sustain the multi-faceted nature of the work of the centre, a nature that has grown, incrementally, over time.

Each worker considers how she or he came to be involved with the centre and how a typical day's work for them might look. In this way, the chapter begins to convey the diverse nature of the work and activity that has developed in and around the centre, and that comprises the *heart* of the *heartland*. Later chapters will detail some specifics of this work, but for now let us begin to map out the territory of activity and get some sense of the route from childcare and early education provider to community project through the incremental building of a *project identity* (a term we explain in greater detail later in the chapter).

### Chi Chi: early years worker

'I've worked here for eight years; I started a placement as a pupil in school and I knew it was for me. Typically, I will start before 8 am. I work in the under-5s base. It's really just putting final touches to the prepared environment to meet the curriculum and the children's individual needs. Throughout the day we will follow the curriculum but we will be flexible to change if the children want it. We have to accommodate children who have particular needs, or carry through monitoring under a court order and complete logs for our social workers to complete reports. We do daily observations, weekly reports and more lengthy assessments monthly, three-monthly and six-monthly, and play plans, so we do a fair bit of planning and review.

'We might get called upon to help in a family's domestic situation; we try to refer across in the service but sometimes we have to do what's needed because the family will only want us because they have a relationship of trust with us. Often, we're the access point for families. They might initially present with childcare issues but, as they get to know us, it transpires that they need more support and it's a way in, so we all work across disciplines and are seen as equal. We also do workshops on language, numeracy and literacy with parents and other carers. There are also daily meetings with parents. We do have to do court reports and go to court on child protection cases. We also do home visits and help parents with behaviour or play skills, or just to share and co-work with them for the benefit of the child. Visiting homes can put people at ease as it's more comfortable and they've got more control. We can work better between the centre and home in a partnership approach, especially on concerning issues.'

### Mohammed: early years worker

'I've been working here for eight years. I used to work in Pakistan in the camps, and then I met Jenny when I was working there and I was recruited through that. I was studying at the same time as I was working in the camp. I was teaching the early years.

'I start at 8 o'clock so I'm usually here for 20 past 7. I have overall responsibility for the 2s to 5s so I'm not just in one unit. First thing I do is check everything is all right. I take over if we have any shortages. We have parents coming in to talk. Some have issues with their partners. Yesterday I had a parent coming in – the partner and her had split up and she asked if she could discuss this so I took her in the meeting room. She was telling me that if the partner came, we couldn't release the child; there was violence and the child had been distressed. She stayed for a while and sat with the child, and I spent an hour or so talking with the parent, going through it all, she was telling me the problems. Then she went away and the father rang two hours later wanting to see the child. Again, we didn't have anything in writing or a court order so if a parent comes on the premises and wants to see a child we have to allow that parent in and get in touch with the partner. I had to inform the mother that he had rung and was coming down. She was at work and distressed and I had to ask her what I should do. We agreed I would supervise him while he spent some time with the child, she said she would come as well but didn't want to be in the same room. The father came and spent time with the child. I didn't feel uncomfortable with him 'cos he was fine playing with the child. After an hour, we were getting ready for lunch and he left. That was the end of the problem but it needed careful handling.

'I usually eat with the children, most of the staff do, and then we take it in turns and some go for a break. This child was fine. After lunch we stayed inside as it was raining, and did some work on animals. After that we had dancing and someone had a birthday and we had a disco. It finished for me about 8 o'clock. We often have problems, like the taxis didn't come in time, parents are late; sometimes a child has to be taken into care. I usually lock up.'

## Daljit: play therapist

'I've worked here for eight years. I joined the early years service and because of the work went on to do play therapy qualifications.

'A typical day – what's that? Nothing is typical here. You never know what's going to present itself or happen. It's the nature of the service. I do have standard appointments, either group or individual, and I work with the children in their bases. Some of the work can be court linked but mainly therapeutic. I can take a non-directive approach most of the time but I have used more direct forms and sand play therapy. I also work alongside the play workers to help children who need it to develop their play skills, and with parents on playing with children. I also deliver therapeutic play and do talks and presentations.'

## Carol: worker with older people

'I've worked here for ten years. I was taken on to work with older members of families using the centre, but my work has expanded since then.

'I get involved with individual older people and groups of older people. Because families are not just about younger people, we are trying to show, so that from the moment you come through the door you see all different ages, races, a mix of men and women and people with disabilities. It's important that older people are included in this. On a typical day I might do some reception duties to welcome older people, we do a lunch club for older people so I help with that, organise trips, organise shopping and food, we do events and workshops. I've been encouraging older adults to share their life experiences with younger ones. We've got older people as mentors. I organise and help with the contact scheme for grandparents because it's sad really when grandparents don't get to see their grandchildren, and the grandchildren and grandparents suffer. We do reminiscence sessions and older people help the teenage mums with advice, just being there as an adopted granny or grandad. It's very popular. We link to "Better Government for Older People". I do fundraising and refer to statutory services for help. I organise funerals and help with preparing for death with other workers in the centre. We've bought graves for older people because it's a real issue, they may not be able to afford it and are concerned about being put in a pauper's grave. We have a respite scheme for those caring for an older person. We might get them on a course in nursing care, using our training provider partner. Oh and advocacy is a key one; our work can interlink at the centre.'

### Anya: mental health support worker

'I've worked here for one year. I applied for the job and was successful in interview. I knew of the work of the centre before.

'A typical day involves group and individual work, attending meetings to support people with mental health problems, helping with individual needs like shopping, self-care skills, medication, providing opportunities to talk, encouraging access to leisure and recreation, visiting hospitals. There's also an advocacy role and it's about co-working with other workers. The focus in my work is on prevention and mental well-being, and it can be with children as well as adults. I co-facilitate mental health support groups and attend meetings across the city in relation to mental health. There's a review going on at present and I'm lucky that elements of our work are involved.'

### Jack: men's worker

'I've worked here for about 16 months. I applied for this job as it was an area I wanted to do more work in.

'I always make sure I work with the children on curriculum or playwork alongside the other men and women in the nursery or the out-of-school units to provide a role model for the children and parents, and to encourage the male parents and grandparents to interact more with their children and to encourage men to use the provision. I deal with individual casework or areas of discrimination and advice, and often I do presentations or present papers at conferences. I facilitate a gay fathers' group, a young fathers' group and a grandfather's group, as well as a general fathers' group. Often at weekends I organise trips away and we run parents/grandparents' skills for mixed groups and male-specific groups. I work every day on the national men's database and with children on gender issues in schools or at the centre, so each day changes really, depending on what I'm called on to do.'

*Winston: development worker*

'I've worked here for about two years. I was drawn to the centre's community principles and co-operative structure.

'On a typical day I could be called upon to support existing groups at the centre, maybe the older people's group or the Female Genital Mutilation Group. It might be the multiple-birth group or a drop-in session, a toy library or books for babies, or a childminding network meeting. The development work is to help individuals who come together and want to form a group, applying for grants, helping them with constitutions, although I often refer them across to the legal eagles on the team. I facilitate meetings locally and attend external meetings to represent or to get information to feedback on new systems, fundraising or whatever. The groups and work are all capacity building. I do research for different groups and for the centre. I monitor all forms across all the services; it's important for quality, targeting, evaluation and development.'

*Shakila: women's worker*

'I have worked here for nine years unpaid and one year paid. I got involved when I heard about the centre and the help it gave. There was a woman I was working with in a community centre whose child was snatched by her ex-husband. She needed help. After I saw what the centre did, I asked if I could help as a volunteer.

'Today I visited a woman in a refuge. We referred her. I offered her face-to-face support and checked that her cultural needs were being met at the refuge. I came back and filled in the logs. After this I came back and led the 50-plus women's group; this includes a lunch and fitness session with a discussion/support group afterwards. After this, I picked up on some of the things that some of them needed doing – welfare benefits, hospital stuff etc. – and referred them to an appropriate worker or arranged their appointments at the hospital. After this, I helped a woman whose child had been sexually assaulted, and sorted out counselling and advocacy support for the child and herself. I then helped a woman who needed advice on maintenance orders and took a woman who is a refugee to a clothing store to get clothes for her children at school. I also helped her complete a DSS form, with the help of a translator of course. After that, I finished reports.'

*Toby: welfare rights*

'I've worked here five years and was dragged in [laughs]. The administrator organises my diary. It might involve a range of appointments but we have an open-door system; preparation for tribunals and going to tribunals. The advice given can range from benefits, housing, employment etc. We work closely with the lawyers and advocates as well as the children's workers so that we provide an all-round service: using a buzz-word from team meetings – seamless.'

*Paulette: family support solicitor*

'I've been working with them [the centre] for ten years. I heard about their co-operative practices and got interested that way. A typical day would comprise us getting 8–20 enquiries. I know this because I looked back over the telephone logs yesterday. The primary areas are around family law, human rights, immigration, not surprising nowadays, housing issues, looked-after children matters, criminal matters, which sometimes go on to include negligence and criminal injury. We've been getting quite a bit of education matters coming through. A typical day, say yesterday – it's difficult because no two days are alike here really because of the diverse nature of the service – came in, opened mail, had our morning focus meeting with the chair in attendance . . . one typical case is of a child in care and his family. They want increased access as does the child but social services are limiting this at present and applying supervised contact arrangements. Another one is in relation to someone seeking political asylum. He's been here ten years but the battle goes on. A further case is a mother who alleges rape against her ex-partner. And yet another is a mother who sustained a severe beating witnessed by her four children, who came to the centre – a very complicated case. We're not only offering legal support, we're also wrapping other forms of support around the family as well, like counselling for the mother and children, play therapy and art therapy support. We've given practical support with rehousing and re-equipping a home, helping relocate the children's schools, and in one of our centres, we're overseeing supervised outreach contact support with the father at present . . . it's a holistic approach to helping and to valuing people in all their diversity . . . another issue would be a gender issue, maybe relating to men working with children. A recent example is a bloke who has been working as a nursery nurse for 11 years in a state nursery in London. He has been subject for several years now to overt harassment of a sexual and gendered nature by female colleagues. It's appalling the level of discrimination and the avoidance of the local authority to deal with it effectively. There was an appalling situation at his workplace, which forced him to say "enough's enough". He's left working with children altogether and is doing manual work. His whole life has been what he termed "destroyed". He contacted us for help and we helped him legally and by wrapping advocacy and counselling support etc.'

*Pippa: film-maker*

'I've been working with them [the centre] for nine years. I approached the centre on behalf of an independent film company, regarding a documentary I was making, and I've been involved ever since. Today, I arrived at 9.30 am and reminded the children (this is children in the out-of-school club during the holidays) about the film they had decided to make on listening to children, with a focus upon abuse, and we had an update. I spent time doing workshops, research, scriptwriting, use of cameras and sound, the children made some trial runs. I showed a previous video they had made and they broke into groups to discuss it and how it could be done better, which they applied to this new film they were making. The film is for the Children's Film Festival and to be shown at the [Millennium] Dome and children's conferences. We had a rundown at the end of the day.'

The work of all of these individuals with both children and adults is varied yet interconnected. Growing familiarity with their own and others' work, and with the underpinning ethos of the centre allows the interconnections to become evident to workers; they can then convey this, through their descriptions of their work, to 'outsiders', in this case through the medium of the interviews. Their voices become their story and, collectively, offer a testament to the co-operative spirit of their work. Their collective responses begin to depict a strong sense of the multiple facets of 'family' and of 'community'; of both their complexity and of their self-evidence.

We have heard, for example, how in some cases, the family begins to need more than just childcare/educational provision for their child; as trust in the service and the service providers begins to grow, the complexities of the family's needs become more evident as the adult family members begin to reveal the extent of their difficulties. From a 'simple' family need of provision for the child emerges a more complex family need relating to educational, financial or similar needs, all of which will impact on the child's capacity to progress and develop within the early years provision, and all of which can be acknowledged and responded to by the services that have gradually developed at Sheffield Children's Centre.

We have heard about the very evident needs of a woman experiencing domestic violence; yet the service must consider, too, the rights of the father to maintain contact with the children despite his allegedly abusive acts. It must consider the children's rights to be both protected and, unless a court rules otherwise, to maintain contact with their father.

Within a broader community context, the centre ethos has recognised and sought to accommodate a focus on multigenerational and intergenerational work; this, however, is rendered more complex when racial and cultural dimensions come into play, requiring a sensitivity of thought and action that must be developed, maintained and nurtured within the heartland, a place where values and principles are recognised as equitable and respectful by those who come into contact with the centre. Because of this, they choose to remain associated with the centre in a wide range of capacities, to bring with them their respective skills, knowledge and expertise, and to pool it in support of children, families and the wider community, both geographically close and at a distance. So, the experiences of a male worker in London are seen as just as germane to the centre's ethos and sphere of reference as is the experience of an attending mother and her children. In both cases, the emphasis is on support for choices and for the rights of the individual to live and work without fear of oppression and in safety, regardless of their orientations, ethnicity or culture.

One of the issues that begin to emerge from these reflections is the extent to which the work of the centre and of those associated with the centre inevitably brings them into contact with statutory services and services provided by the maintained sector, most substantially through the local authority.

There is a considerable degree of advocacy work referenced, with several cases indicating possible local authority limitations in terms of not providing helpful responses to the circumstances being experienced. We are not suggesting that any authorities might have been acting inappropriately or negligently at these times, but rather that centre-based and associated services had developed so that staff were able to give a fairly rapid response to individuals and families in difficulty. This is because they operate on a holistic basis from a premise of shared ideology, and because they have come to know which expertise to galvanise on behalf of the individual and families – these aspects are integral to their capacity for being a catalyst for change with participating families. However, we might speculate on the extent to which this could bring the Sheffield Children's Centre into potential conflict with an authority in that the authority might experience some disturbance to its equilibrium over time. This is a central aspect of the ongoing discussion within the book.

## What is meant by a 'project identity'?

Over a period of years, while undergoing both a geographical and an ideological transition from the church hall as a community programme, to an established children's centre co-operative located in an inner-city area, close to the city centre, the Sheffield Children's Centre has evidently expanded from a temporarily funded childcare and educational provider to a community-based service offering multiple provision parallel to, or wrapped around (to use government parlance), that of childcare and early education. As the book unfolds, we see the centre workers providing for children within the requirements of the Children Act and in relation to the early years curriculum. We see them offering practical advice for addressing family difficulties, including legal advice and advocacy support. We see them offering support groups and personal development programmes to parents, grandparents and carers – in effect, developing and expanding their family support services. We see them promoting the interests and perspectives of both adults and children, sometimes in extremely sensitive areas such as domestic and child abuse.

In all this, the centre involves service users, adults and children, along with service providers in decision-making about future directions. In this way, through the work of the centre, the disenfranchised are given a voice. They are seen by those who come to work there and, as will be revealed in later chapters, by those who use the services, within and beyond the local community, to be taking a non-judgemental and a culturally appropriate approach to their work. We begin to explore this from service users' perspectives in the next chapter to complement this initial focus on the perspectives of service providers.

The works of Castells (2000, 2004) and Calhoun (1994) are helpful in establishing the relevance of the construct of project identity to the work of the centre. They consider concepts relating to *social influence*, *social change* and the place of *identity* for groups that are attempting to influence changes in society. It might be recalled that, in their early days as a community programme, the staff working in the church hall had begun to take account of comments from some community members that the local nursery school seemed not to be acknowledging their cultural and ethnic identities, and they felt that this was having a detrimental impact on the children's experiences. Castells describes a similar phenomenon in the following way:

> people resist the process of individualisation and social atomisation, and tend to cluster in community organisations that, over time, generate a feeling of belonging, and ultimately in many cases, a communal cultural identity. I introduce the hypothesis that, for this to happen, a process of social mobilisation is necessary. That is, people must engage in urban movements (not quite revolutionary), through which common interests are discovered and defended, life is shared somehow and new meaning may be produced.
>
> (Castells, 2004: 64)

Urban movements, as Castells refers to them, or social movements grow out of the desire, by ordinary people, to influence social change based on local demands, to redirect patterns of activity towards their own beliefs and ideals, even if these may appear in the first instance to conflict with those of the perceived majority. In the case of childcare and early education, we see parents and carers aspiring for cultural reference points for their children, within the service provision. Understandably, they are reluctant to consign their children, and more especially their very youngest children, to services that ignore or diminish (deliberately or inadvertently) their cultural heritage through non-representation. Social movements emerge as ordinary people begin to get organised and seek to influence social change from a non-formal social space (Delgado, 2006).

Within society, there are groups that not only create and conserve discourses but that also push for social change in direct ways; the former may evolve into the latter quite slowly or more quickly, depending on the groups' capacity for articulating and sharing their aims and goals, on their cohesion and unity, and on their shared beliefs around a view that some differences are being made – for the better. Minority groups can then seek to oppose what they see as established norms. In this way, they gradually become innovating agents. As Sheffield Children's Centre developed, so it began to impact on emerging policy through dissemination and debate (more on this later in the book).

Minority groups, of which many of the workers at the centre are members, because of the centre's recruitment policy, do not necessarily see what they are doing as exceptional but rather see it as an integral part of their social and cultural life (Mugny and Perez, 1987). They may implicitly or explicitly recognise that a sense of collective empowerment and appreciation of social diversity enhance community cohesion (Morrissey, 2003). Simply by emerging, active minorities change the balance of power and undermine the status of established norms; they begin to create a collective identity that comes into ascendance, and attract and are attracted to other projects and identities that connect with their perspectives and actions. They seek a right of recognition (Satterfield, 1996) and work jointly in a sustained process. This does not necessarily mean that the group has a composite identity but intra-group differences are accepted as part of the group, not because they have been imposed, but because the group's norms have broadened (Moscovici, 1976). Their aims and goals can be multiple but interconnect through the shared identity, although this identity is likely to have many facets. We have revealed something of these facets with the reflections from workers reproduced above, and will build on these as the book progresses.

It would be misleading to think of the community served by Sheffield Children's Centre as homogeneous; there were then and continue to be multiple groups connected to the centre, locally, nationally and internationally – groups whose origins and identities have shifted over time. While both within and across the groups there are aspects of shared identity and common ground, there are also acknowledged heterogeneous elements to any local community. There is an inherent danger in assuming that particular characteristics relating to lifestyle and life choices predicate automatic association or shared identity. Put simply, 'I may seem like you but I may not think like you or want the same things that you want'; alternatively, 'I may seem different but in terms of our aspirations and goals, we may have more in common than you realise.' And, of course, this is the danger of stereotyping where assumptions are made about solutions for 'perceived' social groups through service provision, when solutions are predicated on beliefs about needs and lifestyles rather than emerging through genuine consultation and participation. Dahlberg and Moss (2005: 79) draw on Levinas's (1987) work to explore these ideas through the construct of 'the Other', an Other who cannot be classified and categorised but who can be respected and for whom we can be imbued with responsibility. For Levinas, the emphasis is on obligation to the Other without expectation of a profitable return, also a key tenet within the co-operative movement. Levinas speaks of 'heteronomy', which means a community that has to be understood in terms of dependency or interdependency rather than in terms of autonomy.

The centre and its work offers both *heartland* and *catalyst* in support of an emerging but always evolving identity within the local community. This combination of heartland and catalyst was subsequently to become the basis of action in a much wider geographical arena for the centre. As the *heartland*, in the early days it gradually drew increasing numbers of individuals and groups into its landscape, in the first instance to access the childcare and early education services that allowed adults to return to work and training but, beyond that, into much broader arenas of activity (as future chapters will show). As the *catalyst*, it began to reflect back to a range of service users a renewed and invigorated sense of their cultural identity by becoming increasingly effective at understanding, encompassing and promoting diversity through its services. One of the centre's underpinning tenets is a fundamental recognition that all aspects of diversity are integral to community life; bringing such a tenet to life is a huge challenge. This is explored further in Chapter 4 and, as might be anticipated, we see there the extent to which this belief tests the resolve of both service providers and service users in their day-to-day lives and work.

Reference has been made to the potential in centre practice for conflict with what might be perceived in the mainstream as more typical practice within provision of this kind. If others locate this fundamental aspiration, their desire to be inclusive, beyond the bounds of what might have been perceived as 'normal' in the community prior to their work, then we see the Sheffield Children's Centre potentially assailed on two fronts: by a local authority with whom it might work in partnership, and by the community that it wishes to provide for in partnership. As far as the local community is concerned, a position emerges where two potentially diametrically opposed forces are at work. One force seeks, as described above, to create a project identity that not only respects, but also mirrors, their diverse cultural lifestyle choices and child-rearing practices. But another identity might be perceived by some factions in the local community that see diversity as a threat to their own established and prevailing influences. This poses interesting questions about the extent to which any individual or group can sign up to newly emerging identities while feeling confident that they can retain a sense of self and self-worth if they perceive their own identity to be differently framed than that of what they may see emerging, in this case around the centre and its work.

Project identities, on the other hand, emerge necessarily from conflict, from local demands struggling to change perceived conditions of exclusion and existing power relationships. In extraordinary circumstances, groups such as the Sheffield Children's Centre not only resist their conditions but also are able to propose alternatives to mainstream views by attempting to reconcile and overcome such contradictions. The story of the centre is, by and large, a history of the construction of alternative ways to engage with the children and families with whom the centre is connected, and with communities within which it has come to be embedded.

Dahlberg and Moss (2005: 171) draw attention to the number of preschools around the world that have begun to address diversity in local need, leading to the offering of differentiated solutions for children, parents and staff; in doing so they have 'opened up difference as a subject of minor politics'. Minor politics is offered as an opposing construct to 'major politics', which addresses the significant issues of society but, as they claim, is equally important in terms of impact on lives. 'Minor politics' brings back into the arena issues that politicians and others might see as technical or no longer contestable; one such issue may be 'difference'. Dahlberg and Moss identify preschools as 'sites for democratic practice and minor politics' (2005: 15) and note that one way of characterising this complex political role is as resistance to power. They also identify and illustrate how preschools have much to offer in terms of a political role, through bringing critical thinking to bear on practice and by confronting injustice (2005: 122). Dahlberg and Moss draw on Sheffield Children's Centre as an example of the practice of minor politics.

Delgado (2006: 66) offers an example of a community-based preschool scheme that began in 1981 in one of the rapidly growing shanty towns of Mexico City. The example is interesting in showing the essentially political links between provision for children and families and the politicising of those who act for social change within this arena. The Mexican initiative emerged originally from links between educational researchers and local mothers at a time when national government had no responsibility for providing for young children and families. There were strong feelings among parents that the few government sites that did exist were largely culturally inappropriate and insensitive. As time progressed in the new initiative, the mothers took greater responsibility for the development and maintenance of services and began taking responsibility, as groups, for particular aspects of service development, but with a strong emphasis on democratic action and development. In time, the external researchers left the project although they continued to support the community and its practice; adjoining projects began to develop including a licensed primary school, and this expanded to the formation of organisations and to publications aiming to provide an alternative to that offered in government publications relating to provision for children and families. The original founders of the work began to gain academic qualifications, and also began to take a wider interest in influencing social change more broadly and to become substantially involved in national changes in the political scene in Mexico. They progressed from being childcare providers to becoming advocates of democratic participation.

This is a relatively brief example of the emergence of a *project identity* in services for children and families, one that grew from small beginnings to have greater political impact, and one that subsequently encouraged local women to engage in national action. In continuing the story of Sheffield Children's Centre's journey to project identity, Chapter 2 considers how the child's cultural heritage, as rooted in the family experience, has become a starting point for service development at Sheffield Children's Centre.

# VALUING CHILDREN MEANS VALUING FAMILIES

This chapter opens by describing the centre's development into an Early Excellence Centre; this initiative was to locate the centre and its work within the national arena, consolidating its growing reputation and further developing its *project identity*. The section that follows illustrates the basis for this growing national reputation in terms of the centre's own policies and practices as implemented and as perceived across the local community and beyond. The chapter goes on to illustrate, through children's voice and family vignettes, how both policy and practice are rooted within a fundamental recognition of the child's cultural heritage and personal experience as an individual, within the family and within the community. This recognition of cultural heritage is a fundamental tenet of the *heartland*; it is the starting point for championing children's rights and for developing culturally appropriate family support, each of which becomes a wellspring for the *catalysts* of social influence and social change within and beyond the local community.

The family vignettes reveal to us the impact of the services from service users' perspectives, extending the viewpoint beyond the perspectives of service providers as seen in Chapter 1.

## Becoming an Early Excellence Centre (EEC)

The EEC pilot programme was launched by the Labour government in August 1997, after the party's return to office earlier in the year. Between 1997 and 1999, 29 pilot EECs were designated in England, of which Sheffield Children's Centre was one. The EEC programme was part of the government's broader strategy for raising standards, increasing opportunity, supporting families, reducing social exclusion, improving the health of the nation and addressing child poverty. The EECs were to give a practical reality to emerging ideas about 'joined-up thinking', where care and education would combine to offer one-stop shops to children and families; a location or a network of service providers where multi-agency, partnership working would emerge and flourish, where good practice would be modelled and where the exemplification of integrated practice could be disseminated, through training opportunities, to other providers (Bertram *et al.*, 2001). Each centre designated its own evaluator as part of the national evaluation programme.

At this time, Sheffield Children's Centre was already a one-stop shop, working in a multi-agency way when it became a designated EEC through an independent submission to the DfES; the local authority had made a separate submission that had not included the centre in any capacity. We have seen in Chapter 1 something of the range of services that had evolved, over time, as a result of individuals either being recruited to or attracted to the service and its ethos. The centre has always been staffed by paid and unpaid workers from a range of agencies and professions; centre workers were already offering a range of training opportunities to other providers, both within and beyond the city, when EEC status was achieved.

Year two of the EEC evaluation at the centre had shown the range of qualifications the workers had already achieved or were working on; these ranged from NVQ Level 3 to doctorate, including graduate and postgraduate qualifications. This second-year evaluation also illustrated the extent of workers' frustrations in that, despite their EEC status, lack of money inhibited the development of services in innovative and, to them, necessary ways. Becoming an EEC gave added impetus to their work and they were coming to see more clearly their own potential for expansion. Their reflective journals, kept during this year, illustrated further frustrations with statutory services in terms of what centre workers saw as the statutory services' delays in responding to children with special needs. As we will see in Chapter 3, centre workers often advocated for children and families, and one expressed her views, via her journal, on how she felt the local authority representatives were responding as a result: 'seeing people I've worked with in social services and other services turn against us ... feeling the weight of the authority on us as a centre because of our challenges to them'. The EEC evaluation would focus, in part, the following year on the centre's relationship with the local authority and we return to this aspect in Chapter 3.

Financial support as an EEC was available to the centre until March 2006. The DfES had also designated around a quarter of a million pounds as contributory towards a new build for the centre. Its prefabricated site had been designated for closure by the turn of the century and architectural plans were commissioned, at substantial cost to the centre, in 2000 for the new build. However, the EEC programme was subsequently superseded by Sure Start Local Programmes (SSLPs) and the income that had come directly to the centre from the government via the EEC programme would be diverted into the SSLPs and ultimately into the local authority in the roll-out of Children's Centres. These policies had the potential to gradually weaken the position of community-based providers and strengthen the role of the local authority in determining the nature and location of services for children and families across local communities.

Chapter 3 takes up this part of the story in more detail, but at this point in Chapter 2, let us move on to examine how policy and practice at Sheffield Children's Centre placed social justice in the *heartland* and utilised incremental flexibility as a *catalyst* for support for children and families, and for developing services.

## Becoming a centre of excellence

The centre has long been recognised as a centre of excellence in relation to its provision for children with special needs and has regularly been commended for its multicultural staff profile. An inspection report from 1997 remarks: 'The cultural diversity of the staff is a great asset and this is reflected in many of the activities the centre offers.' The centre has an active policy of diversity in staff recruitment and this relates to culture, ethnicity, religion, sexual orientation and disability. This is a brave policy, demanding proactive defence on occasion, but in terms of their heartland, centre workers do not see how they can respect diversity in the wider community unless it is reflected in recruitment practices.

Letters of testimony received during the evaluation of the centre as an Early Excellence Centre recognised and celebrated this groundbreaking work in relation to social and cultural diversity. A small number of extracts from the letters are included here to give a feel and a flavour of the scope and impact of the work developed over the years and, in particular, the extent to which the centre's work relating to diversity and entitlement for children and families has been manifest.

In July 2000, the Leader of the City Council wrote:

The centre has extended a wide range of support services encompassing families in the widest sense with specific innovations, going back many years and including:

- The inclusion of children with special needs into mainstream services
- Encouraging and ensuring the inclusion of men as carers of children
- The early integration of education, play and care alongside other family support services
- The development and delivery of a multi-cultural and diverse service
- Delivery of non-stigmatised provisions for children particularly those children in need
- The development and delivery of advocacy support services which sometimes necessitates the Centre challenging the statutory provisions
- Support services for socially excluded groups
- Extended family support provisions
- Representative roles on committees and commissions etc.
- Pro-active child protection services based within a therapeutic and family rights framework
- Advocating for and delivering children's democratic inclusion in decision-making processes
- Work with lone parents and teenage parents

- Provision of services for children and parents who are terminally ill and after care provision

The centre has always maintained the strongest possible position regarding equality of opportunity and social inclusion and has endeavoured to ensure that its services are always culturally appropriate and accessible ... [it] has also contributed to policy development within the City Council.

A community service officer offered this written testament (undated):

As a Community Service Officer I have placed 14 individual offenders subject to court order with the centre. All these offenders completed their orders successfully with a number of them carrying on voluntarily for a while. I think their attitudes, friendliness and professionalism has, in no short measure, made this possible. The staff's treatment of these offenders has always been non-judgemental, welcoming and trusting. I know from offender feedback that these attributes have meant a great deal to them personally. In some cases, some of them have changed lifestyles and employment choices to reflect the experience they have gained while working there.

In May 2003, the Chief Constable of South Yorkshire Police wrote:

Tangible examples of your assistance to the Force are as follows:

- Support for children at risk throughout Sheffield but particularly with regards to the police who work with the community in the Sharrow and Lansdowne areas
- Provision of care and support for children who find themselves in custody through the arrest of their parents or guardian
- Delivery of multi-agency training programmes on child protection issues
- Provision of support for the child and adult victims of domestic violence
- Support for the victims of crime generally, particularly children subject to abuse or assault
- Involvement with the multi-racial racial harassment project by supporting children and families
- Involvement on a South Yorkshire basis in relation to children and drugs and substance mis-use by representing children's views, advocating on their behalf and providing direct services
- Contribution to the Force's Independent Advisory Group and subgroup assisting with local policies on racist/homophobic/transphobic incidents to complement the ACPO Hate-Crime Manual.

These testimonies give insight into the scope of the work within the centre and across the wider community. They illustrate the extent to which the needs of children and young people lie at the heart of service provision, while also recognising that the social and cultural context of the child's lived daily experiences have to be acknowledged and engaged with from starting points of non-judgemental acceptance and of a non-stigmatised service. In order to develop comprehensive and responsive services within an economically disadvantaged community, an uncompromising acceptance of some basic principles for action is required. These are evidenced in the centre's equal opportunities policy of which a small extract is presented here.

The equal opportunities policy for Sheffield Children's Centre states as its aims:

1. To combat racism and discrimination in all its forms;
2. To create a positive and welcoming service and environment for all;
3. To positively encourage people from a wide variety of backgrounds to work in partnership with the centre;
4. To challenge attitudes, procedures and practices which create barriers to using or being involved with the centre;
5. To make individuals aware of their role in implementing and supporting this policy.

The centre's extensive policy document continues:

**Why is this policy necessary?**

All children, adults and families, plus communities should have the opportunity to access, take up and receive the services we offer and to achieve just and fair outcomes for themselves, irrespective of their colour, race, nationality, ethnic origin, religion, gender, marital status, sexual orientation, age or disability.

Unfortunately there is evidence to show that individuals are discriminated against in many walks of life. The existence of equality of opportunity cannot be taken for granted.

Organisations must put in place special arrangements to ensure that the users of their services, or members, are treated fairly and in a manner that results in positive outcomes.

Legislation is in force to prevent discrimination and to promote equality of opportunity in many areas of social life. The Sheffield Children's Centre however not only wishes to uphold the letter and spirit of the law but to adopt best practice in management and delivery of services.

With regard to equality, the centre works towards the elimination of discrimination and to promote equality of opportunity. But it recognises that it is essential to extend this remit to deal effectively with other forms of disadvantage and discrimination.

The policy continues for several pages, demonstrating in tone and content an uncompromising acceptance of the challenging and ongoing nature of implementing such a policy. The next section illustrates how the principles are put into practice, in the first instance, as a normal part of daily activity aiming to give voice to children's experiences and desires. This is followed by family testimonies on the impact on their lives of their links with the centre.

## Championing children's rights

As part of the Early Excellence Centre evaluation in year two, a questionnaire was designed by children and young people to find out how their peers felt about the centre. Such evaluations are common within centre practices. The one from which the example below is taken occurred over the holidays as part of the out-of-school activities.

### What would you and your faimly [*sic*] do if you didn't come to the Centre?

*Find another place but it would be hard because lots of places don't want kids like me.*
(14-year-old boy with cerebral palsy, of English heritage)

*Try and find a place for me to go but we will not find a centre as good as this.*
(4-and-a-half-year-old boy, of Chinese heritage)

*My mum would probably give up her job to look after me.*
(11-year-old boy with brain damage, of Pakistani heritage)

A total of 24 children responded on this occasion; several were helped by older children and adults. The respondents ranged in age from 3 to 14 years; they represented 16 cultural heritages, some having dual or triple heritages. In designing the questionnaire (with adult support) the children had included the question 'What is your culture?' Cultural heritage is seen as an integral aspect of personal identity at the centre; children and young people are encouraged to recognise and talk about their heritages as well as being supported through resource provision across the centre's services. Ten respondents had identified a special need – another of the questions, and another key aspect of personal identity inextricably linked to entitlement and personal wishes.

The selected comments above illustrate, in the first response, the child's sensitivity to how adults elsewhere have responded to him. In the second response, we see an example of how a quite young child can have a clear perspective on 'quality' in relation to their personal experiences. In the third response, an understanding of the wider implications for the family if they were not receiving centre support at this time is expressed. The selected comments help us to see that children of all ages understand the world around them, and have a view on how they are perceived and received within that world – a view that the Sheffield Children's Centre is helping them to articulate and, if necessary, to challenge.

It is now acknowledged more widely that children and young people are experts in their own lives and they can operate as competent participants in research and evaluation (Langsted, 1994). When suitable forms of engagement are provided, they make substantial contributions to knowledge, both about their learning processes and their well-being. Clark and Moss (2001) advocate a 'mosaic of methods' that draw on familiar experiences for the participating children, and Armistead has illustrated its use with quite young children (2004, 2005). These methods might be conversations, questionnaires, focus groups, tours of their settings – the key is that the methods are complementary, that they are age-appropriate and, as the Children's Centre approach has illustrated, that they are culturally sensitive in respect of ethnicity, race, religion, family lifestyles and disability.

Research with children and young people needs to be child/young person orientated and not adult orientated; they must be seen not as subjects or objects but as equal participants, (Woodhead and Faulkner, 2000). Quite young children can express a view on what constitutes quality for them in their daycare provision, even though the word 'quality' may not be in their vocabulary (Armistead, 2005, 2006). As Mayall (2000: 120) points out:

> Children constitute a social group, a permanent feature of society and thus their knowledge of what it means to be a child and what it means to children to engage with adult individuals and adult social groups is needed as part of the task of improving our understanding of how the social order works.

The UN Convention on the Rights of the Child has been influential in the movement towards children's participation and voice. The Convention has 41 articles directly relating to human rights. Article 12 states that parties shall assure the child the right to express views freely in all matters affecting them; their views must be given due weight in accordance with their age and maturity. Article 13 gives them the right to freedom of expression. Article 30 gives them the right to enjoy their own culture, to profess and practise their own religion and to use their own language.

In England, the Children's and Young People's Unit called in 2000 for greater participation by children and young people in influencing and shaping local services and in feeling valued and being heard. In drawing attention to these policy shifts, Prout (2003) demonstrates the extent to which children's conditions and experiences of childhood have shifted in the last 25 years, suggesting that previously held tenets and practices no longer apply; there have been huge cultural shifts in children's lives and many children now play and learn in multicultural, transcultural and diverse communities. We would argue that it is only in recognising the fundamental inequalities in society as a starting point (Baker *et al.*, 2004) that the true power of diversity finds voice and impact.

## Culturally diverse families and culturally appropriate support

Let us move on to listen to the voices of adult service users, in order to gain further insights into the lives and experiences of some of the families being supported by the centre's services. As with the children's responses above, these extracts also came from EEC questionnaires during 2001. A total of 71 parents and carers responded to the following questions:

- Can you briefly describe how you have been helped by Sheffield Children's Centre?
- How did you find out that the centre could help you?

- How do you feel that you and your children have benefited from using the centre?
- If you had not had the support of the centre where do you think you would be?
- Can you think of any other support that would have helped you?
- Do you feel that you have learned any new skills?

Many respondents were experiencing, or had experienced, difficult circumstances, as shall become evident. In presenting their voices here, we run the risk of projecting a view of the centre as responding only to those in the greatest need and this is by no means the case: a whole cross-section of society uses the centre and its community-based services. However, the weight of these testimonies is especially important in making explicit the extent of the need, for families, where life is lived on the margins of society or, as discussed in Chapter 1, in a state of social exclusion through poverty and related difficulties. It is important to acknowledge the extent of the need that continues to exist within society. What the testimonies also do is define for us how the Sheffield Children's Centre meets those needs for adults, young people and children. In this, we begin to see the flexibility and responsiveness that underpins the services, and that arise out of the non-judgemental, non-stigmatising ethos that they have worked so persistently to engender and that pervade the heartland.

The centre is recognising and acting upon a belief that it is virtually impossible to support the child's rights to equal access and to a high-quality experience unless support is also offered for the family unit as a whole. This is an underpinning principle that supports its continued existence as a community heartland. For some families, an effective, high-quality childcare and early education service is only a small part of their need; as stated in Chapter 1, it is what is wrapped around this core service and, possibly more importantly, how that 'wrapping' looks and feels to service users, that begins to make the most substantial difference as they seek to make changes for the better in their own and their families' lives. As noted previously, the Sure Start Local Programmes that followed on from EECs were premised on a construct of reaching the 'hard to reach': those who traditionally did not access services. In such a designation is an inherently assumed deficit that community members are at fault, rather than that the services might be culturally inappropriate.

The forthcoming testimonies depict a small part of the range of need being met. Some were compiled by workers with service users, when, for example, respondents did not have the literacy skills or confidence to commit to paper but who wished to be included. The responses were all powerful and moving, and it was difficult to select examples from the full range of those available.

Reaching a decision about how to present these 'family vignettes' has required considerable discussion by the authors. We wanted to avoid any manipulation of these testimonies but wanted also to ensure that they were accessible and meaningful for a reader. We reached a decision to omit the questions as presented above, as they fragmented the vignettes. Where additional words relating to the original questions were needed, to sustain continuity, these have been added *in italics* to distinguish them from verbatim responses. Spellings have been corrected and punctuation added.

The vignettes have been grouped to facilitate an illustrative commentary, which is presented at the end of each grouping. This is potentially misleading in that it might suggest that particular characteristics are not only discernible from others but are in some way more significant. While our aim is to be illustrative of family contexts, it is not to oversimplify human experience. In the first vignette of the first grouping, the mother's lack of knowledge of English and England are issues to be addressed for her; while this is also the case in the second vignette, we see there that a family bereavement is also supported. In vignette 3, horrific family experiences in Somalia are integral to family identity and aspiration and, in vignette 4, the children are taken abroad by their father to the country of his birth, against the wishes of their mother and against the law. So while these four cases are connected by ethnicity and culture, it is the family experience within the lived context of ethnicity and culture that the centre workers aim to support, and not ethnicity and culture as distinctive features.

### Family vignette 1: the Khan family

'When I came to England I could not speak any English. The centre helped me translate formal documents and make applications. They fought for my children and gave the school support with my children, with language. I went to their "English as an additional language" lessons and sewing classes, and I'm doing an NVQ in childcare.

'*I found out about the centre* through the mosque.

'*We have benefited* with English and with helping us to settle into England. It is not too scary, having them there, and they give us confidence.

'*Without them I'd be* stuck at home reliant on my mother-in-law and husband.

'*I've learned* English, education of early years, using a sewing machine and how to live in England.'

### Family vignette 2: the Ali family

'I visited the centre at first to talk to the solicitor about immigration matters, and then asked for a place for my toddler, who attended three days a week. At the time I was seven months pregnant and in the eighth month I went into labour. I went to antenatal classes at the centre and the pregnant women's group with aqua aerobics. My baby was stillborn. The centre staff advocated with the hospital for us for care of our baby's body. I am a Muslim. They also arranged for me to go to a group for parents who lost their children through stillbirth and early infant death. Counsellors supported me and my husband, and when I became pregnant again they helped me through fear and the pregnancy itself. Now we have another healthy baby who goes to the centre.

'*I found out about it* through my sister, who had got advice on an immigration matter.

'My little boy has learnt English more quickly and can play well with other children and has learnt so much. We would have been lost without their help when our baby was stillborn. They had a strong sense of our culture and helped the hospital to understand. They did training afterwards and the hospital was much more sensitive. They also gave us the confidence to get through the next pregnancy, and to cry about our baby because it was all right to.

'Our religion is important to us and we were so lost when our baby was stillborn and we couldn't speak for ourselves, and they made it all OK. I'm sure I would have been really depressed without their support. They helped us make sense of what had happened and gave us hope to carry on.

'Nothing can prepare you for the death of your child and the centre couldn't have helped us any more than they did.

'I've gone on to train on a foundation counselling course at the centre, on grief management, and have signed up for a Diploma in Counselling so that I can help families who lose a child. I can help in the support group for families like us now. I have done talks in the Pakistani and Bangladeshi communities to break down the taboos.'

### Family vignette 3: the Jama family

'My mother was pregnant and we had to get help from the centre when she was going into hospital. We have 14 children in our family. Ten of them are my two aunties' children who died in the war in Somalia. The centre gave us home workers to help us and to take the little ones to school. They were Somali and they helped us with lessons and play schemes and nursery places. They helped her after she came out of hospital because she has arthritis and they still help now.

'Isaac told us about it.

'We've got proper help and the workers know our way of living 'cos they are Somali as well, and we couldn't all go to school and we got to go to school to play, and we didn't get split up.

'*Without them it would be* social services because who wants 14 children?

'*We've learned how to* play new games and sports, how to use a laundry and iron properly. *We're* better at maths because workers helped us with homework.'

### Family vignette 4: the Oubi family

'I had a nervous breakdown after my husband ran away with my two children. He took them to his country of birth on a contact visit. The children had gone to the centre from being little. The centre helped me with legal advice and put me in touch with women like me. Because the staff are from different cultures and the centre works with different countries, they were able to make contact with the right people. And they located my children for me. Staff went over to bring my children back with the support of the government there. And they counselled me and my children throughout the process. The staff from my husband's culture help the children with cultural lessons and teach the language so they see the best in both cultures they come from. They helped me when I had a breakdown by giving me a mental health support worker who was there for me throughout it all.

'I used the centre for childcare and learnt more about it that way.

'We are strong and we are one again. Words cannot express how much we have benefited; only the angels know. Each day I wake up and see my children's faces and hear their voices in our home. It's a benefit only a mother would know.

'I would not have lived without my children. I honestly know. I would have killed myself; living without them would have been unbearable.

'*I think* the police could have helped me.

'The centre has encouraged me to help and support other women, one in a situation like my own, and this has made me more capable to give presentations, fill in inter-country reports, know the legal system more. I've decided I want to be a children's family solicitor and the centre helped me find a suitable course. They're supporting me with childcare. They also put me in touch with the other mothers in higher education and we've set up a support/learning group to help each other, make lots of new friends.'

## Illustrative commentary

It is very evident across these four vignettes that word of mouth is a common way for centre users to come to know about the centre services, suggesting a substantial amount of trust of the centre across the community and particularly among its most isolated members. Adults learn about the centre from other adults and from children. The ethnic and cultural diversity among the workers enables the worker team to have knowledge and understanding of specific cultural issues and needs on a wide basis. Service users come to understand this, and this helps trust to develop.

The centre networks are wide and can operate community-wide, country-wide and internationally. The response to family need is neither judgemental nor stigmatised. This is supported in some cases by the centre workers' own life experiences, some of which are similar to those of service users, and which come to be recognised as such by service users because the workers are happy to talk about their own periods of difficulty. There are no hierarchical boundaries across workers and service users.

The next four family vignettes illustrate how terminal illness and bereavement are also an integral part of the centre's support services. Their services extend from cradle to grave as death is seen as integral to life's journey.

### Family vignette 5: the Andrews family

'I'm terminally ill and a lone parent with three children. The centre has been a lifeline for me. They help me with respite and by giving the children chances I can't give them. They've been helping the children understand that I'm going to die soon, and have been helping them make plans for this and for their future without me. They take the children to see me in the hospital

for their foster parents and they let them meet with other children who have lost their mother.

'I was referred through the hospital. When you're facing death, it's very frightening when you have children. Having the centre involved has lessened this fear and has given me some comfort to know that the centre will make sure they are kept together and given choices.

'*Without the centre I would be* at the mercy of social services.

'*I have learned* how to die with dignity and to share that with my children.'

## Family vignette 6: the O'Hara family

'My wife died and we've got six children. I could not manage and was going to put them into care, when the centre helped me. They put in a home worker and gave children places at the centre. I was to carry on working. They sent someone to do the laundry twice a week, and help me with the shopping when I need a break. Sometimes they send a childcare worker so I can get out on my own. They've taken the children away for a holiday to help them mix with other children who lost their parents.

'The hospice asked them to help us.

'I was able to keep my children and get through the upset.

'*Without them I would be* drunk in some gutter without my children. I was heading that way. *It would have helped* to have had the centre involved earlier while my wife was alive. I have seen how they help other families when the parent is dying; we needed that help but we did not know about the centre.

'*I have learned* how to be a mother and father, housekeeping skills, how to show my emotions and how to play with my children without feeling daft.'

## Family vignette 7: the Benson family

'My ex-husband took our children out on a normal visit and he killed them and then he killed himself. The centre got me through it. I was suicidal. I couldn't carry on and the centre stepped in. The children had been at the centre. They came to me and shared my grief. They dealt with the press for me, and they helped me rebuild my life and showed me that I could live a kind of life and help others.

'*I knew about the centre* from day one of the children going to nursery. They were not just a nursery, they were a family. It sounds "chichi" but it's true. When my ex-husband was causing trouble, when we separated they helped us through it and asked for a risk assessment on him because they felt he might behave irrationally. The assessment by statutory services never came and they put pressure on but it was too late for us. He was a professional, middle-class man. The mainstream felt it was me being irrational. The centre, because of its work, knew different.

'The children developed really well and walked and talked quicker. They know more about other religions and cultures than I did. They fostered caring and empathy in them. My husband was encouraged to join a fathers-only group but he declined. After their deaths I was helped therapeutically and I have moved forward.

'Without hesitation I can say I would have terminated my life just to get to my babies.

'It changed my life for ever, and the skills of compassion, support, advocacy and protection I learnt from the centre I now use in my daily work as a bereavement counsellor. The centre helped me get on a diploma course and funded my fees on short workshops on Child Bereavement and Violent Death. The centre is full of reminders of my children, at first too painful to face but now I go there for comfort and to help others like myself.'

## Family vignette 8: the Dewhurst family

'My husband died and I couldn't afford to bury him. As well as that I just didn't know what to do. The centre helped me to organise the funeral. They got money from the social and they fundraised to pay for the rest of the funeral. I'm an old age pensioner; it would have been impossible.

'My home help told them about my situation. He would have been in a pauper's grave by now. My husband fought for this country in the war and worked all his life in the steelworks. We're not moneyed people. They are helping me sort out my money now and plan for when I die because it really worries me.

'I don't know where I'd be *without the centre. I've learned* money skills.'

## Illustrative commentary

Children and adults are supported through their experiences of bereavement through explicit and open acknowledgement of their circumstances. There are no attempts to shelter and protect children from the truth, but shelter and protection are evident and take the form of knowledge and understanding through discussion and through meetings with others in similar circumstances. Workers support families in maintaining daily family life in practical but non-intrusive ways and through periods of considerable difficulty.

With ongoing support and a parallel sense of forward-looking, individuals can be helped to surmount what may seem at times to be the most overwhelming of personal circumstances. But, beyond this, they are able to then use their personal experience to support others like themselves, through the warp and weft of the centre's network of ongoing care and compassion. The centre's work does not recognise age as a barrier to access to services when responding to need in the community.

The next four family vignettes address issues around mental health and domestic violence, illustrating further how the warp and weft of centre services encompass the whole family through the provision of flexible and responsive services. These vignettes also prompt considerations, as of course do many of the above, of what the implications might be for all these individuals, adults and children, if family life were to cease through family disintegration because of these difficult circumstances.

*Family vignette 9: the Kerrigan family*

'I have had mental health problems. My kids have gone into foster care and the centre has given them stability and brought them to see me. When I'm home with them the centre helps them with things like shopping, taking me to hospitals, they keep a check on us, give the kids a lot of breaks and go to hospital appointments as well.

'When social services were thinking of putting my kids up for adoption they helped me. My kids could be in care full-time and they are not because of the centre, and they keep an eye on me through the mental health workers [support]. The kids get a lot of support going out on trips and visits, with their housework, chances to play, chances to talk with the counsellors to know why I'm sick and what it means. *Without the centre I'd be* in an asylum!

'I wish that I could have known about them earlier. I don't think I would have gone into the hospital under a section.

'I've learnt play skills at the centre and how to play with my kids. I've learned how to ask for help and how to manage my sickness.'

*Family vignette 10: the Stanley family*

'As a child, I was sexually abused by my father. Only when I had my own daughter did I confront this and I went to the shrink. The centre gave me one-to-one support and I joined the adult survivors group. This made sense of my fears for my daughter's safety.

'I saw a leaflet about the centre and its sessions and I just turned up. It brought me back from going over the brink with my mental health. I was having flashbacks and panic attacks, and was overprotective with my child. It helped me come to terms with everything and I have come through it. *Without the centre* I would have been over the brink.

'*I could have been helped with* a service like this as a child where I could speak out and be listened to.

'I've definitely got better coping skills and have learned that parenting is not just about protecting your children but allowing them to take risks so that they can develop and learn to protect themselves.'

*Family vignette 11: the Malik family*

'I came to the centre for help with domestic violence. They found us a refuge and went back to the house to get our things. My husband left the country after this and they found us a house in Sheffield and helped us furnish it. They got us school placements and gave us a baby place in the nursery, and they got me a place on an access course in college. My children go to the children's group and the violence support group. Everyone knows it's the place to go for help. They never turn anyone away.

'The centre has kept us alive and safe, and it has helped us get over the violence. He would have killed us. In our community there is no escape and it is expected that women stay with their husbands. The centre gave us a different path to escape, and the cultural workers made it OK with our community.

'Now I am a single parent I have had to learn lots of new things and I'm at college on an access course so that I can get a career to look after my children. My three boys have learned it's wrong to beat women and hopefully they will not do it to their wives.'

### *Family vignette 12: the Bowden family*

'Two of the children go to the centre nursery and the other one goes to the play scheme. I ended up in hospital after my boyfriend assaulted me, and the centre took care of my children and helped them through it; they developed terrible hair loss and my body was weeping with psoriasis and I went back into hospital. Again the centre looked after the children with their child-minders. They found me a new house and helped us more and we all got counselling for the domestic violence. They helped me through the court case and I've been able to open up a beauty parlour with their help. They gave me business support and advice and they helped with publicity. I'm doing well and so are the children.

'*I found out about the centre* from the newsletters. I was conscious of the services but I never thought I would need anything other than childcare. We came through all the difficulties and we made a new life. I've always wanted to have my own beauty salon but I never thought I could do it. The centre staff pushed me to do it and gave me support. It has helped us financially as well, having this new salon.

'We're alone in Sheffield and the children would have gone into care while I was in hospital, which would have been my worst nightmare. I lost my confidence and I would have ended up in terrible depression. The court process was also a nightmare. I would have withdrawn without their support and he would have come back to me.

'My children learnt that no matter how frightened you are you have to stand up to bullies, whoever they are. They see me as a strong woman now and I've learnt to be strong. I've learnt business skills, book-keeping, administrative skills, by going on courses and getting one-to-one tutoring from the centre.'

### Illustrative commentary

There have been numerous examples of centre workers 'walking alongside' families in difficulty, prepared to make the journey with them, over time, and supporting and encouraging their sometimes slow but nevertheless forward movement out of their difficulties and back into a fulfilling, if still challenging, life. There are no quick fixes. Immediate practical help sits alongside the possibilities of forward movement; in fact the forward movement could not emerge without the immediate and flexible help.

Alongside the word of mouth mentioned above, we see the promotion of services attracting new clients to services. But, as before, it is apparent that huge trust must underpin the decision of a woman, abused as a child, to make use of services relating to her experiences that were advertised in a leaflet.

The final four family vignettes examine a range of family circumstances affecting both adults and children. Once again, the immediate and longer-term responses by workers to these families illustrates the wealth of knowledge and experience that they are able to draw upon, sometimes from their own lives, as a result of a fundamental commitment to creating a heartland that provides a catalyst for change and growth for both workers and service users.

### Family vignette 13: the Lefrette family

'I am blind and wanted to return to work after my maternity leave. The centre took my child and helped me throughout with childcare. It helped me to provide stimulation for my child, not just in the nursery but at home, and gave us a chance to be a normal family with invites to social events. My child is now at school and uses the out-of-school facility. She has a strong understanding of disability issues and she is very accepting of differences. The centre helped me to have confidence in my parenting abilities.

'*I found out about the centre* through talking to my midwife and health visitor. One of them had two of her grandchildren at the centre and the other regularly referred children. *We have benefited* through giving us equal access. It limited intervention from statutory support, which I was unhappy with because of the stigma. It normalised our life and increased our experience. *Without the centre*, I think our life experiences would have been much more limited, and we would have faced discrimination in access and acceptance which, in turn, would have a negative effect on my child's self-esteem, identity and confidence.

'It's hard to quantify *what new skills I have learned*, but I think help with parenting, given my sight restrictions, was really an important skill, and learning from other mothers and staff of the centre who had sight impairments gave me lots of new skills as well.'

### Family vignette 14: the Wong family

'I am HIV positive and so is my child. The centre has been a lifeline to us. It has given us respite and accepted us with open arms. It provides us with normality and warmth. The wide and diverse services are always open to us and I regularly have staff accompanying me to medical appointments as well as advocating for us for increased support.

'We knew that the centre was an inclusive place via its reputation in the community and we approached them to see if they would allocate a nursery place initially. After that we joined support groups, alternative health clinics at the centre, and dance and language workshops. All of this has embellished our lives. It has helped me to carry on and to see myself and my child as part of a bigger community and family – that of the centre. It has taken away from the feeling of being alone, and specially trained counsellors have helped me come to terms with the terminal illness we face and helped us to forge ahead with plans for different contingencies. When I have felt low, the centre has sent in home support, has kept us together; whatever is ahead of us, we know we will not face it in isolation.

'*Without the centre* God knows *where we would be*. I don't think we would have got the help elsewhere. Services would have been spread and some of them just don't exist anywhere else. Where else would we have been emplaced with such compassion and acceptance, and valued for what we are? We're not statistics or stigmatised, but seen as unique and of value at the centre. *I have learned*:

- how to live is a skill they gave to my child and myself
- communication skills across cultures
- to use IT, in workshops at the centre
- my child is fulfilling her learning potential and has a quality of life because of the centre
- I'm doing a signing course at the centre so that I can communicate with people who are deaf or hearing impaired
- yoga and meditation skills, and I'm doing a course on visualisation techniques on Wednesdays at the centre as well.'

### Family vignette 15: the Camerra family

'My 12 year old had a baby. The centre protected the family from the press when it got out, and helped us with maternity services and social services. They gave our daughter childcare and antenatal lessons, carried out helping with school lessons, gave counselling to us all, helped the baby get things, helped my daughter get out of the house. The support worker was there at the birth to get her and us through. They gave presentations at school and the youth club on teenage pregnancy. The baby goes to nursery at the centre and our child got into a new school with their help.

'Our daughters' friends told her *about the centre*.

'*We were helped in that* the stigma is terrible and it is hard for a child to carry a child, and for us as a family to see her go through this. Pressure was put on her to give the baby up for adoption. She didn't want to and the centre helped her keep the baby.

'*Without the centre we would have been* at the mercy of the state.

'*It would have helped us if there had been* less judgement from the community and more understanding. We never thought this could happen to us; we're a religious family. Our daughter learnt how to be a parent and the responsibilities that go with it the hard way, which was softened by the centre, who recognised her for the child she is.'

### Family vignette 16: the Alahabi family

'Sheffield Children's Centre helped our family because our middle son was on drugs. They got him a place in a clinic and got us rehoused and had police protection put in because we were getting threats. They went down to the pawn shop and got back all of our belongings my son had sold. They gave us access to counsellors and they liaised with the police for us.

'*We found out about the centre through* word of mouth. They help lots of families like ours. It has saved our family. We were on the brink of disaster.

'*Without the centre* my son could either be dead or killing other people with drugs, and our family would have been destroyed.

'Earlier interaction in the schools and drug awareness training for all children from an early age *would have helped. I have learned about* drug awareness and nursing skills.'

### Illustrative commentary

The term 'one-stop shop' seems barely applicable to the wide range and type of assistance that centre workers have become able to harness over time in support of individual families. In each case, they introduce the parents and carers into agencies and groups that deal with the immediate difficulty and also extend potential for both adults and children. Word of mouth remains a key information point, and it can be seen to be operating among young people as well as among adults.

Through their work and services they take the personal problem into the wider environment, through knowledge and information for other community members. This can be preventative but also anonymously supportive for particular individuals in difficulty within their own local communities because of their current circumstances.

### Chapter summary

These powerful and personal narratives illustrate how the interweaving of family lives, difficulties and triumphs can rest at the core of a child's experiences and possibilities. We might conceive of these as the 'voices of the oppressed', as discussed in Chapter 1 where it was noted that such voices must be heard if new and successful norms of policy and practice are to be manifest. What these voices tell us is that 'oppression', while engendered by circumstances and lack of opportunity, can be powerfully confronted through new opportunities and renewal of empowerment. This empowerment comes through word of mouth, and through connection with and access to a pervading and well-connected infrastructure of culturally appropriate support and engagement as a right, rather than a 'gift' or a 'policy'. In these circumstances, the 'oppressed' become the new innovators of developing practice.

The centre and its services have evolved over time to move far beyond the narrow confines of a statutory curriculum or of targets to reach the 'hard to reach'. Alongside these families' struggles for survival (literally in some cases) and the discovery of the wherewithal to overcome seemingly insurmountable difficulties, we can see the impact of the encompassing but gradually liberating services of the Sheffield Children's Centre; we can see it becoming an urban movement reflecting common interests and experiences, and creating a shared pool of enterprise and problem solving.

The capacity for a flexible and non-judgemental response is evidenced time and time again, and this becomes an integral part of the centre's work as *catalyst*. When parents, carers and children engage with that response they not only feel supported in seeking to surmount their difficulties but they return in many cases to re-engage with the services, bringing their new strength and knowledge with them as inspiration for other families, and as continued growth and contribution for themselves, their children and their local community. This reciprocity is an integral part of what helps the service to grow and develop as a partnership rather than from a perspective of reaching the 'hard to reach'.

When children see their parents and carers become strong through adversity they too know and understand more about human possibilities, and this then becomes strength for them and for their contribution to the wider community and wider society. They move from being dependants within that *heartland* to become contributors and sustainers of the *heartland*. Their strength is the community's strength, and represents a strength within the wider society also.

# A COMMUNITY CO-OPERATIVE: GROWING AND SUSTAINING THE SERVICES, AND THE TENSIONS IN BEING A CUTTING-EDGE PROVIDER

As Chapter 1 described, funding for the community programme provision established by a Labour government was ended by the Conservative government on its return to power in the early 1980s. As well as the desire by government to locate greater responsibility for 'children in need' within the local authority, subsidised jobs in local communities were perceived by some as a threat to expansion within the private sector. The Children Act 1989 had rendered the church hall where the service had become established non-compliant, so the workers and service users, together, as a management committee, secured a new location for their services, close to the inner city and continuing to serve the same local community. In this introductory section of the chapter, we look at the national context for childcare and early education evident in the latter part of the twentieth century and providing the broader context for Sheffield Children's Centre's emergence as a cutting-edge co-operative providing services for children and families.

The management committee recognised the need to expand their services in order to remain financially viable. From near closure would emerge a unifying identity for their work, an identity that would reflect their shared intentions for a socially just society; one that could help them to remain a catalyst for change in response to community needs and experiences, and in conjunction with the local community. In this, they were acting in accordance (albeit unknowingly at the time) with Castells' (2004) theory of urban movements, as discussed in Chapter 1. The workers at the centre, along with service users, were becoming cohesive and unified by their common experiences, goals and strivings; the previous two chapters have illustrated this emerging cohesion through responsive action and interaction. Their internal discourses were pushing for social change within their shared social justice agenda, and this was engaging the centre workers in advocacy activities as the discourses became external; they sought to change wider society to reflect the unrepresented cultural norms of the groups using the centre. In this, then, they act as a catalyst for change for service users and for the wider society; they are becoming innovating agents in promoting social diversity through enhanced community cohesion (Morrissey, 2003).

From a time of difficulty and uncertainty about their future would emerge a stronger service, a cutting-edge service that, as Chapter 2 has shown, would already be well established once Labour government policy caught up in the late 1990s. However, in Chapter 3, we also consider the difficulties and uncertainties that continued to prevail for the centre in some aspects of its relationship with the local authority.

In the late 1980s and into the early 1990s, Sheffield Children's Centre was to enter a new era of income generation and of financial management. This was to be an even more challenging era for it, as Jenny's comments in Chapter 1 have already illustrated: 'There have been times in the office when we wanted to cry . . .'. Relocation was not only to be a geographical act; it would present a timely opportunity to re-vision the service and to consolidate its progress from childcare provider to community provider reflecting the community ethos. Its work as *heartland* and *catalyst* was about to expand, and this expansion would be what placed it favourably so as to receive its Early Excellence Centre designation. Fortunately, Jenny, one of the founder members of the centre who had come to work in the original community programme, also had a background in accountancy, and with the move and the centre's new aspirations she drew on this knowledge to expand her role:

> So when we moved to this building, they needed someone to do personnel, so they sent me on a course for personnel and then I went on the Montessori course and I went on the Advanced Play Course and then I went on the Child Protection and so forth . . .

In 1989, the management committee had developed its Articles of Association and this embedded their future development within the co-operative ethos. Chapter 1 has already illustrated the extent to which provision for children and families was well placed to flourish under the co-operative principles at this point in time. In the late 1980s and early 1990s, funding for services for children and families was already coming from a mixed economy of public funding and voluntary activity. Private-sector involvement in these services had not reached its present levels but was beginning to emerge as increasing numbers of women began their return to work.

Within the maintained sector, responsibility for provision for children under school age had devolved to local authorities with the Education Act 1944. However, it had never, until relatively recently, been statutory and as a consequence, provision around the country had evolved as patchy and unequal. We saw in Chapter 1 that the Conservative government at this time clearly considered childcare to be a parental responsibility and so the climate for change was not conducive. A local authority could close nursery schools and nursery classes without any community consultation if it felt that its budgets could not sustain existing public services. The majority of local authority provision, by way of nursery classes attached to maintained schools and the far less common nursery schools, would have been provided predominantly for the lower-income communities by Labour local councils. As a consequence, it was these communities that subsequently suffered most substantially from closures.

The Children Act 1989 had given local authorities responsibility for providing services for 'children in need', but definitions of need remained a grey area and had little impact on overall levels of service provision across local communities other than the buying in of places for children in need within existing services by social services departments. A statutory entitlement to early years education for 3 and 4 year olds would not emerge until the Education Act of 2002. At this time, the Labour government gave a 12-and-a-half-hour entitlement to all 4 year olds and later to 3 year olds, finally and for the first time breaking away from the premise that early education and childcare were private matters and finally acknowledging, as many Scandinavian and European countries had for many years, that the state has related responsibilities.

The playgroup movement had emerged in the 1960s with mothers (mainly) seeking to fill the gap in local services with what they hoped would be a temporary initiative, which gained its strongest presence in relatively affluent suburbs for many years until government funding allowed expansion into less affluent areas (although it is debatable just how successful this expansion has been). Overall, the playgroup movement's expansion across the country has undoubtedly been successful, with 9000 groups registered in the mid-1970s (Kellmer and Naidoo, 1975) and some 15,000 currently registered.

When Labour took power and began the series of reforms that would lead to the establishing of Children's Centres, there were well-established and numerous testimonies to the fragmented nature of services for children and families in England (Baldock, 2001; Cohen and Moss, 2004). Bradley (1982) and Pugh (1988, 1990), prior to this, had been calling for the integration of services being developed respectively by the community and voluntary sector, the private sector (small but about to grow) and within the mainstream sector, provided separately by education and social services. They, and others, had repeatedly drawn attention to the need to integrate services for children and families, and the implications of doing this for local authority structures of government, and for national government structures and organisation.

When the Sheffield Children's Centre moved to its new premises and then ceased to be the St Mary's Community Programme, the country was still several years away from the integrated services and substantial changes to local and national government infrastructure that would follow on from Labour's election to government in 1997 and from the later emergence of Children's Centres from government legislation. The Children's Centres, emerging in 2005, followed on from the Sure Start Local Programmes that had started in 1999. The Early Excellence Centres had been designated from 1997.

Sheffield Children's Centre preceded government initiatives by more than 15 years, both in name and practice.

## Becoming and being a co-operative

This section offers a brief focus on the co-operative movement to illustrate how Sheffield Children's Centre, as a *heartland of influence* and a *catalyst for change*, both within and beyond the local community, began to flourish and expand within a co-operative ethos. The co-operative ethos gave the centre a framework within which to operate, a framework that reflected the collective commitment to service development at the heart of its activity.

In the early days, the workers delivering on the community programme had not been actively seeking social change; they had been striving to provide a service. It would also be true to say that, even today, many of those who work at the centre see their main focus as providing services within their own community and, in some cases for some of the time, for their own children. They do not see themselves as 'changing the world' nor of having a *'project identity'*; their work moves on from day to day, centred around the education and care of the youngest children, and engaged with families, carers and the wider community.

However, their constant exposure to, and willingness to address, the injustices and severe difficulties experienced by many of their service users (and sometimes by themselves) has gradually politicised long-standing workers, both paid and unpaid, to the extent that they hope for alternative ways of being and for a more general sense of hope and happiness for community members. A growing sense of solidarity allowed a shared identity to emerge in the form of a social enterprise – or project – and this social enterprise or project identity would be nurtured by the co-operative ethos.

The International Co-operative Alliance provides the following definition of the identity of co-operatives, a definition recognised throughout the world:

### Definition
A co-operative is an autonomous association of persons united voluntarily to meet their common economic, social and cultural needs and aspirations through a jointly owned and democratically controlled enterprise.

### Values
Co-operatives are based on the values of self-help, self-responsibility, democracy, equality, equity and solidarity. In the traditions of their founders, co-operative members believe in the ethical values of honesty, openness, social responsibility and caring for others.

### Principles:
- Voluntary and open membership
- Democratic member control
- Member economic participation
- Autonomy and independence

- Education, training and information
- Co-operation among co-operatives
- Concern for community

(Co-operative Action, undated: 146 for expanded version)

We have seen evidence of these values and principles in action from the voices of previous chapters and now add one more voice to this testament: a conversation between one of the authors – Pat Broadhead (PB) – and a parent. This parent and her children have travelled a long distance in their family journey with the centre, as her reflections reveal. In the early part of her narrative, Lisa (pseudonym) reflects without interruption from PB and, towards the end, a conversation ensues. Her extended narrative reiterates many of the illustrative comments from the previous chapter and provides more detail about her own and her family's journey with the centre, from dependants to key contributors, both for herself and her family. Lisa also conveys an understanding of how the centre ethos, as expressed through its leadership structure, is integral to the conditions and climate that allow the centre to flourish, to develop its services in the way that it does and yet to stay true to its social justice principles. Later in the chapter, we will focus more substantially on the conflicts that begin to emerge for the centre as its services and success grow, but first we need to examine in a little more detail how its co-operative ethos has shaped its identity as a community provider.

## Lisa's journey

**Lisa:** Around 1989 I was getting a lot of negative attitudes from society. 'You've got yourself pregnant, you haven't got a man.' I went into a deep depression, at one point I tried to kill my daughter, I nearly threw her from an 11-storey building. I realised I needed help, and contacted my social worker. She knew of Sheffield Children's Centre when it was in the church. My daughter started there and everything began to fit into place. A few weeks later I went for an interview and was offered the job and it was a darned good job. I did part-time study and went on to do a university access course. Then I got pregnant again and I got my baby boy. The Children's Centre was once again there. They never judge me for what I did in my life. I'd got support in the days, at weekends, in the evenings if I had meetings. I went on to do a degree and then got my master's.

I should step back a bit because before I got to where I am now, I got in with the wrong crowd and the wrong kind of environment, with drugs and everything. Now I'm totally against drugs but I was still supported through this time. Now I feel I have something to give back to the community in developing anti-racist issues, political aspects. If the centre needs legal advice I'm here to help them.

My son has had father figures in the male carers here. He expressed his views to them in a masculine way.

My daughter is now involved in working with the children's groups here; she has become a leader with them. It has boosted her. She's met David Blunkett, spoken out on videos, she is splendid.

Helping me has allowed me to help them, it's like full circle. It's a learning curve, you learn, you help them. This community is so multicultural, not only do they help the kids and the families but it influences the community as well. Any way they can get help from the community enables the centre to become more effective within the community.

If it wasn't for the centre, I would have been dead or in jail and my kids would have been dead, totally, they would have been. I'm working now, got enough money, but they're here supporting me still. I've got enough money. I'm having little problems right now, which I'm trying to rectify.

I've seen how they manage children. You know, kids are fighting or whatever: they say, let's paint, let's do something, take them out on the field for football. If it weren't for the centre, my kids would never have made friends with the calibre of people they have. My son has had learning and hearing problems. He is head of his football club; he won awards a couple of weeks ago. He was playing football here and the manager saw him. He spoke to several people who said he was good and he got him into the team. He's 8. My daughter's 11 and still comes here. She loves it; this is an extension of home.

**Pat Broadhead:** Have you any sense of how the centre is managed?
**L:** I don't really know how the place is managed but I know how it operates. M, J and S (founding workers) are at the heart of it. It's a very flat structure, everyone is aware of important information in the staff. There's a lot of sharing information it seems to me. If you need information, they know who to contact.
**PB:** They seem to store and use and share information in appropriate ways. It's not like other models. In other organisations, information stops at certain points because of the hierarchies.
**L:** Precisely. Also you know that, if you get too much information, it can go against you, it can have negative effects. There can be security problems. But that doesn't seem to happen here. Information stays within the centre when it needs to and no one judges you.
**PB:** I think there are many informal opportunities for sharing information and in hierarchies they have, say, a staff meeting for sharing important information and they don't happen too often so lots of information seems to get lost. With a flat structure, there's a more explicit awareness of the need to share information.
**L:** The staff here can communicate at all levels. It's flexible; it changes for each individual, to help. It's dynamic. It helps the community and on a national front also. It works at all levels. We have social events in the evening. It was one of the carer's birthday party and we all went out. You never feel either superior or inferior here. It's a great environment to be in. There's no solid boundary around it. They have, kind of, dispersed boundaries. It changes shape or structure as it needs to.
**PB:** It's as if they say; here's a problem, let's sort it and move on. They don't seem to recognise organisational boundaries.
**L:** That happens all the time.

A key part of the centre's capacity to be effective is, as Lisa sees it, the workers' inclination and ability to 'communicate at all levels' and to relate service provision to individual needs at key points in time for a particular child and her or his family. Key points in time are likely to extend over a period of time for families in difficulty, as has been the case for Lisa and her family. Only with hindsight, when she has moved on from her difficulties is Lisa able to recount the nature and persistence of the centre's work on her behalf. Their *heartland* has created and sustained a *catalyst for change* for Lisa, without the need for targets or overt management. She was not 'hard to reach' because she came to trust the support available to her. No one presumed to know what she needed, but were able to walk beside her and her family as they moved forward, gradually, out of their difficulties.

The centre's structures allow it to envelop Lisa and her family and, in time, from being located within the *heartland* they became a *catalyst* for change *for others*. But Lisa doesn't see it as 'their work'; she sees it as their caring and non-judgemental engagement with her, a sense (also perceived with hindsight) that they believed she would make it through these massive difficulties, even through the darkest times of drug abuse and potential child harm.

For centre workers, this would have not been an easy task; they must always keep the child's safety and well-being at the heart of their actions. Their difficult work is helped by worker solidarity rather than by the hierarchy of managerial responsibility, by a shared understanding of a social duty to Lisa and her children, their willingness to take a collective responsibility for the whole family, and their firm belief that neither the well-being of the child, her or his parents or of society is served by removing a child from its family home unless absolutely necessary. Some workers at the centre have themselves overcome difficulties with the support of the centre and they understand the nature of the journey and of the support needed. They understand that the best interests of the child and the family are served by providing a warp and weft of support for all family members – of people, of services and of beliefs, underpinned by clear communication channels and a non-judgemental approach. These are the principles of social justice in action, hugely challenging but ultimately beneficial it would seem.

It would be inappropriate to call this work 'an intervention'; the centre workers did not 'intervene' in Lisa's life. The centre's structures and day-to-day operation allowed centre staff to encompass Lisa and her family in a continuous and supportive way just as it did for the many families whose testimonies were presented in the previous chapter. We would argue that this stems from its underpinning values of self-help and self-responsibility within the co-operative ethos, not as 'judgement', but rather as 'possibility', within a context of social responsibility and caring for others. We propose that it constitutes a directly opposing model to the one encapsulated in the term 'hard to reach'.

Lisa can visualise and conceptualise the work of the centre and has become a member exercising autonomy and independence as her own confidence as contributor and participant has grown. She began supporting other parents in difficulty, on a voluntary basis, working within the centre to bring her own experiences to bear in support of their difficulties. In addition, she subsequently qualified as a lawyer and, as she references above, is now able to offer legal advice to the centre as and when it needs it. Reciprocity of this type between service users and service development is a central part of the growth and sustainability of the centre, bringing dignity back for individuals, cohesion back for families and new contributions within the wider community.

One way of envisioning this is to place this reciprocity at the heart of the heartland, to see it as the pulse that drives the project identity, as well as being a key characteristic that builds the shared identity. Service users become service providers by drawing from their own strengths and experiences, something that was never expected of the 'hard to reach' of government terminology. For Lisa and others, their previously difficult circumstances have become their areas of expertise, and this feeds back into the co-operative enterprise and into the channels of communication because of the pervading co-operative ethics and values. It becomes a key part of service sustainability.

The term 'sustainability' has only recently entered the co-operative vocabulary (Co-operative Action, undated). It is a term borrowed from environmental activists to reflect the fact that enterprises that fail to change or adjust to new conditions in a competitive market can become wasteful of resources. Sustainability means growing to an optimum size – large enough to achieve economies of scale but small enough to remain participative and engaging (Co-operative Action, undated: 29). As Sheffield Children's Centre became established on its new site and as its services grew, through word of mouth and through active promotion, the business side required greater consideration. We have seen from the voices presented so far that many service users were not well placed for purchasing services; the staff needed to become expert business planners as well as continuing to maintain and develop their ever-expanding services within a co-operative ethos. We have already heard from Jenny, a former accountant turned childcare provider/personnel/finance worker within the centre, and one of her reflections articulated the precariousness of day-to-day provision within the community sector, lacking as it does the cushion provided to mainstream services. Let us hear a little more about the financial uncertainties the centre has faced on its journey.

## Financial viability: a key issue for community-run services

Earlier in this chapter we talked about the Children Act 1989 requiring local authorities to provide for children 'in need'. This resulted in the buying in of places that Jenny refers to below, a key factor for the centre in relation to financial stability at that time but, as she goes on to describe, this strategy also had, inherent within it, the potential to compromise its social justice principles. Jenny begins by reflecting back on the early days:

> It was very demanding and worrying for the people because there was no guarantee it was going to survive, going to be financially secure. In childcare, it's a very dicey business, if you don't have people that will sponsor you or pay salaries, it's very difficult because you have your children here, the children leave, they go abroad, they go to school, so you could lose ten children in a week and ten children are generating

daily income for you. And you're carrying a lot of free children as well; these children need a place to stay, need accommodation. But we created problems for ourselves. They [Family and Community Services within the local authority] would buy in six places for children at risk but we would become close to those children and their parents. So when another family needed that place, rightly they would put another family in that place, but we wouldn't let the others go. So we accumulated more children than were being paid for, say twenty and only six were being paid for ... we still had the staff to pay, we still had everything else to pay for, so that would acquire debts for us ... it certainly wasn't a money spinner ... in the early days we were working for 50 pounds a week, doing crèches at the weekend, doing all the training we could and it was very difficult ... people left but then they'd got good qualifications from the centre, so we generated a hell of a lot of jobs over the years.

Jenny is reflecting on a key issue here relating to finances in the centre, but also to its desire to retain the integrity of its heartland – both factors in relation to sustainability.

Towards the fulfilment of legislative requirements in the city, Family and Community Services provided income for six children 'in need' to be located in the centre. When Family and Community Services deemed other children to be 'in need', and the 'need' to have evaporated elsewhere, centre staff were expected to cease providing services free of charge to the previous families. Knowing the extent of their actual need, and, having built close relationships, they could not bring themselves to do this, despite the financial burden they knew it would place upon the centre as a service provider. Here was their solidarity and conviction put to the test.

In a letter dated 10 June 1999, the Chair of the Management Committee of Sheffield Children's Centre wrote to a named service manager in Family and Community Services to indicate that 28 children were currently being provided for in relation to the six paid places. However, additional funding was never forthcoming. Here we see another major difference between the practices of the centre and those of the mainstream. Sheffield Children's Centre does not see itself as responding to 'children in need'; it provides for community members with whom it develops and maintains relationships of support and communication, leading in many cases to mutual and reciprocal support as families become stronger and seek to give something back to the community that has supported them through their difficulties. We will return to this financial aspect a little later in the chapter, but in building the picture of the centre's relationship with the local authority we will consider other aspects of its advocacy work on behalf of community members.

## Cutting-edge provision: a vulnerable beacon in a changing world

In pursuing a social justice agenda for children and community members, the centre workers have, on many occasions, found themselves advocating on behalf of those community members with mainstream services. Mainstream services may not have had the flexibility to operate in the way that the centre did because of the bureaucratic structures that govern them. Several of the vignettes in the previous chapter demonstrated family frustrations at slow and, as they perceived it, ineffectual responses by public departments. Indeed, it is this lack of 'joined-up thinking and action' that led to the death of Victoria Climbié and to the subsequent and massive restructuring of government departments, of local authority structures and of local services for children, families and communities. The *Every Child Matters* agenda has now acknowledged the detriment of public services that work slowly and in isolation (DfES, 2003). The Childcare Bill 2006 requires local authorities and their partners to provide integrated early childhood services that involve fathers, mothers and main carers in service planning and delivery, and that include proactive outreach work. But all of this was yet to come when Sheffield Children's Centre workers were advocating for children and families.

At the turn of the century, the climate in local authorities was different and regular advocacy by centre workers for families in difficulty potentially contributed to a deteriorating relationship with the local authority. In this section we present a small number of additional family vignettes, drawn from the original questionnaires, to illustrate some of the advocacy activities that centre workers undertook on behalf of the families they were supporting. The vignettes have been edited to focus on the context for the advocacy initiatives and to illustrate how the centre was to become more vulnerable at a time when its policies and practices should have become a beacon for national and local policy.

## Vignette 1

In this first vignette, centre workers challenge the housing department under the requirement of the Race Relations Act to assist this family in need.

'Our house was attacked by racists. They tried to burn us out and the centre brought the police in and the racial harassment project to help us. They got us rehoused into a safer area and counselled us through the trauma. They also went into the estate to do race awareness workshops, which has helped the people like us living there.

'We are now free from fear for our safety and have a much nicer house in a safer area. We've also come to terms with the racist attack. The housing department did hardly anything to help us until the centre got involved and forced them to help us under the Race Relations Act. The council and the police could have been more protective.'

## Vignette 2

In this second vignette, the parent is reflecting on the centre workers' stance in continually drawing attention to a racist attack on their son that had taken place in the city centre.

'My older boy was battered coming through town. A group of men did it. They mistook him for a Kosovan refugee (we're Bangladeshi). The centre has supported us in all of this and has raised the matter everywhere. My son was on life-support for weeks. He came off it recently for two days but he's gone back to the machine in intensive care. The centre helps us with the after-school with the children so that we can be by his side. They take the youngest to school and to hospital, and they give them nice toys in the after-school. The translator keeps us up to date with the medical jargon and the centre is liaising with the police daily.

'One of our younger boys goes to the Shack (see next chapter) and he told them about us. They just turned up and asked what we wanted help with. Nothing is too much trouble for them. The centre is a co-operative and it shows.

'There should be more action against racists in Sheffield. No matter how hard you try, you can't protect children from evil.'

In the two similar vignettes that follow, centre workers have supported the parents in confronting the local authority in relation to arguing for and securing a statement of special educational need for their children. Once a statement is acknowledged, there are financial implications for the authority in support of a child's statement.

## Vignette 3

'My son had a learning disability and they helped him with his dyslexia. Jack is now doing really well at school. The Sheffield Children's Centre helped us argue for a statement for him and they got him a place with a specialist teacher and gave us a place in the Dyslexic Support Group at the centre. Jack was getting really disruptive at school, and his behaviour changed and his confidence.

'We've seen other children excluded like Jack. An earlier statement would have helped but the Education Department never told us our rights. The centre's had to do that.'

## Vignette 4

'My child was born with cerebral palsy and the centre from the start included us and helped us with childcare support and help with the special needs process. They assisted us to form our part of the educational statements and advocated for us for the school of our choice. They also fundraised for us to go to the Peto Institute and they employed specialist staff to support conductive education.

'We knew other parents who had chosen the centre for their children who had special needs. We have been made, from day one, to be included as part of the centre, which has helped us to feel wanted and included. We've both been able to continue work and the centre has increased our awareness of disability issues and our child's rights where limits have been placed on us by the state. Staff have come together to advocate for us and we're never alone in our battle for our child and the support he needs. The centre made much needed respite available for us all and gave our son inspiration because he has positive role models in the staff, some of whom have disabilities. Some of them were once children at the centre.

'They have met financial costs for us, of placement, because if you have a child with a disability this is much more costly and the centre is excellent at supporting where barriers exist.

Sheffield has a limited disability budget and our child would definitely not have the support he needs and deserves. We're both in low-paid work and couldn't afford the expensive provision. The pressures on our marriage with the early start of our son's condition were helped by the support we had to make our marriage stronger. Our son's mobility increased because he is encouraged. He has able- and disabled-bodied friends, and is part of a vibrant and rich community of people who are all different in their own way.

'The centre does not get enough state support. The centre taught us about legislation and our rights, and gave us the confidence to meet our child's needs.'

## Vignette 5

In this vignette, the parent tells of advocacy with a local school in relation to bullying of her children and with the Local Education Authority to support a transfer to another school.

'My husband is in prison. The centre has helped me getting through the legal situation, which was frightening for us. They helped us with the schools because my children were being bullied because of other children. They went to the educational appeals panel to relocate one of our children because of problems.

'We were referred to the centre by social services when the children were little and they helped us a lot then as well. Without them the children would have gone into care and, after their dad got into trouble, a whole system wrapped around us to help us understand and get through it.

'It's been a rock for us all and helped us to keep contact with my husband. The distance prisoners are placed is ridiculous. The children wanted to see their dad and the centre helps us so much with this. They protect us from the stigma and keep the children on the straight and narrow with lessons and sports coaching and trips. Our family would be in pieces without them. I go to the centre's art and craft workshops and have been doing art therapy for some time, which has helped me to get rid of upset because I was going out of my mind. Some of my work has been exhibited during a recent art show in Sheffield.'

## Vignette 6

This grandparent recalls advocacy in relation to the Family and Community Services department within a local authority and is herself clearly aware of the resulting hostility towards the centre because of this action of its part.

'The centre has helped me to fight to keep my grandchild. My daughter is mentally ill and my newly born grandchild was taken away under a Section 47 investigation. The centre's cultural advocates helped me put together reports on why the Carer's Assessment Act was not carried out and why a pre-birth and post-birth assessment wasn't either. They helped me understand the jargon and process, and fought for me and my family to get access to our grandchild. We had our older grandchild in the centre 16 years ago and it helped her to develop and learn, and we were able to get custody of her with their help.

'Our family have been able to rear our grandchildren with their help and to get our views across in statutory settings. Social Services should have been less hostile to the centre advocating for us. We learnt how to get through the legal systems with their support, and to know our rights.'

This advocacy work illustrates the growing levels of knowledge and understanding that centre workers were gaining in relation to legislation, and in relation to the rights of children and families. They are using this knowledge, alongside their links with unpaid parent-workers such as Lisa above, to support the rights of minorities, of children with special needs and in other areas. In each case, they empower parents and carers to confront bureaucracy and demand an entitlement; in each case this resounds financially across the local authority. Officers are required to engage and intercede, and not from their own volition. Their principles and personal experiences do not allow the centre workers to act other than to empower individuals with knowledge and support.

Not all centre workers are necessarily actively involved in the above work; it is the more experienced and long-standing workers who have gained the requisite knowledge and confidence, over time. However, other workers are party to the related discussions and centre-based activities because of the flat management structure and the open lines of communication and, gradually, they too become knowledgeable and confident; this is an important part of their own professional development within the centre and a continuing part of the centre's sustainability in terms of renewing the *heartland*.

It is important to put advocacy activities in context; although these and other instances occurred over time, they represent a steady 'drip-drip' of potential confrontation with a range of departments within the local authority.

In the next section, we return to the developing relationship with the local authority, reflecting first of all on the previous discussions around subsidised places for children in need and looking at this from a perspective outside the Sheffield Children's Centre. After that we examine some of the more recent difficulties experienced by the centre workers in relation to the local authority.

## The centre and the local authority

In Year 3 of the EEC evaluation, local authority officers and elected members linked to the development of Children's Services were invited for interview by the evaluator (PB). The links between Early Excellence Centres and the local authority within which they were located were an integral part of the evaluation and some of the emerging case studies have already been used above to illustrate the potential impact on that relationship of advocacy by centre workers. In addition to officers and elected members, other individuals, involved in local authority service development but not directly employed by the authority, were also interviewed. The interviews were taped with their permission and transcripts were sent to them for any comment to be deleted or added as they wished. They were assured of anonymity. These transcripts provide some illuminating data around the relationships between the authority, authority-based service development and the Sheffield Children's Centre.

One officer of the authority responded as follows in relation to the places for children 'in need' discussed above. S/he identified the difficulties arising from these informal arrangements and from what is acknowledged as poor communication:

> The City Council has provided money to the centre to provide a number of full-time childcare places. It's not been done on the basis of a clear contract and I think it's one of the issues that has caused a problematic relationship between the centre and the City Council, the lack of clarity, the lack of a link person within the local authority who can communicate with them when there were inevitable difficulties but there's also a lack of clarity about what's expected on both sides. I've taken this over recently, the responsibility for the contract, not just because there are difficulties but because we are reconstructing all our contractual arrangements. We consider the centre to be a preferred provider so that they are what we would describe as one of our key partners. They've recently won an open competitive tender, a contract to do contact work for us.

S/he identifies the centre as 'a preferred provider', indicating good standing arising from its work as being recognised by the authority. S/he identifies an intention to improve communication. Later in the interview, this respondent commented as follows, confirming a view from centre workers discussed above about the substantial difficulties being experienced by the families that the authority refers to them for support and services. S/he acknowledges the unique aspects of the centre's established provision and also indicates some of the perceived limitations of local authority services at this time:

> Sometimes we might have families that local providers won't work with because they are seen as a problem family and the centre is very good at taking these children and working positively with them. There's the multicultural, multiracial dimensions of their work, which is not evident in all providers ... they have a record with us of being able to provide for children with special needs.

Later in the interview, the officer confirmed the impact of advocacy activity:

> I know the staff at the centre feel that they have been discriminated against and badly treated on occasions. I think part of that is because Sheffield Children's Centre does advocate on behalf of the families they

work with. They do that in a pretty robust way, which creates an uneasy relationship. Sometimes, when we've looked into things, we think things have been said that are not quite right so if there's a criticism of a foster carer we may carry out an investigation and we may not agree with the concerns.

During these interviews, one non-authority respondent spoke of service development in relation to out-of-school provision. This had been at a time when this provision had been newly emerging on the national scene, in relation to childcare provision for children under the Children Act 1989, where the legislative provision for children in need extended to age 16 years and included out-of-school provision. Local authorities were looking to rapid expansion of services for before- and after-school provision and, because of the limitations of their own bureaucratic processes, they were looking to community providers to support this expansion. This period had coincided with a period of expansion and related issues of sustainability for the centre on its new site and, for a period, the centre staff had been at the forefront of developing services in relation to the Out of School Network that was emerging in the city. The centre had been contracted to provide some of the services.

This respondent suggested that, while the centre may have been moving too quickly in terms of providing services in this area, it was also an area of both national and local difficulty in terms of service development and, moreover, the authority was unable to fulfil this demand from its own service provision. Jenny offered a related reflection:

> In the early days when we were generating the money, the Out of School Network had started when we were a community programme and we had our staff servicing various out-of-school provisions. We'd pay the staff and then bill the out-of-school provisions at the end of the term. Our staff were running everywhere to try and generate money to feed back into the system. Problems arose trying to generate finances and finances and finances. And the staff were also doing crèche working, feasibility studies, business plans, working in child protection areas, contact centres, any way we could to generate money...

An interview with a senior officer from the local authority also made reference to this issue. She offered two comments that shed further light on these difficulties being experienced by the centre and the authority response to this, but then reiterated the wide recognition across the authority in relation to the distinctiveness of services: these two contrasting aspects, when juxtaposed, illustrate the tensions for the centre in terms of external perspectives on and perceptions of its development and practice.

This first quote relates to responding to complaints about the centre relating to the out-of-school provision in its early days. This senior officer had previously been talking about positive aspects of centre provision and continued:

> I've been with a different hat on where I know there have been complaints. It's difficult when complaints are made because the registration

and inspection team have a dual role, on the one hand being supportive but they are the first port of call for complaints. While I haven't been directly involved in investigating a complaint, I have been involved in trying to reconcile some of the aftermath. I have gone with staff and parents to evening meetings.

While the local authority must fulfil its responsibilities in such cases, the view is inevitably only partial and full evidence must be sifted. However, any complaint, even those that prove unfounded, leaves a shadow. Despite these short-term difficulties over out-of-school provision, this respondent still recognises the uniqueness of the service and its ultimately vulnerable position in relation to the local authority because of some aspects of this uniqueness:

We're lucky it exists as it offers fairly unique services in the type of roles it fulfils around family support and special needs. It supports children from ethnic minorities, it offers an advocacy service, and that range and diversity isn't equalled in any establishment. There's a lot we can learn from but I think it's important to recognise that sometimes these various roles bring it into conflict with the local authority.

In concluding this discussion, for now, relating to links with the local authority, we draw on a quote from a respondent who worked independently of the authority but who contracted much of her work from it, and who has also had links with the centre over a number of years. She 'sees' the world from the perspectives of the authority, while also acknowledging the ethos and aspirations of workers at the centre, given the substantial and complex needs of a relatively high proportion of its service users.

Here, she captures the 'clash of cultures' as the worlds of bureaucracy and community collide, and gives insight into why the service might be both respected as cutting-edge yet also subject to complaints, and ultimately vulnerable. She is speaking about the early days of service development at a time perhaps when centre workers did not fully understand the perspectives that others might have on their practices, and the impact of these perspectives in certain quarters:

You go into the office and in the office there's five children and a baby on someone's knee playing with a typewriter and another fiddling with the phone and one on the floor with paper and to an Under Eights Officer, that's dreadful because they're meant to be doing meaningful activity within the health and safety of a proper environment. But to them [centre workers] it's like an extended family. It's about cultural understanding and concepts of childhood. Sometimes children are engaged in very different ways with the family. I always felt we should be looking at that in relation to some of these tensions. People turn up [at the centre] and they've got a problem and they [the centre] deal with the problem. We don't do that in society. No, you have to go over there. There's an issue about professional practice and what is seen to be professional.

The final sentence captures the heart of the matter in terms of the potential for conflict between the centre workers and the bureaucracy of local authority practice and responsibility; it is a fundamental ideological conflict. Centre workers aim to reflect and build upon familiar experiences for children; they have a view, in some cases based on their own personal experiences, of familiar family life experiences that will bring security for vulnerable children whose families are in difficulty at this time. They seek to make their practice culturally appropriate and to, in this case, replicate home-based environments for children. More recent debates are now exploring these issues in relation to children's experiences in their childcare and early education settings. The debates build around the centrality of social pedagogical understanding (Prott and Preissing, undated) – that is, of understanding the child's learning processes in the context of their cultural experiences in the home and wider community, and the need to take account of these in constructing and sustaining early learning environments. Burchinal and Cryer's study (2003) supports the view that quality childcare should reflect the cultural heritage of children. Gillies (2005) is critical of policy that depicts 'exclusion' as a perceived disconnection from mainstream values and aspirations, as opposed to being a marginalisation from material resources. Tacit moral judgements form the basis of determining what constitutes appropriate support for both adults and children, and these judgements result in a top-down projection of values and standards on to families, thereby supporting conformity to a predetermined norm rather than promoting access to parenting resources to match families' needs. Once again, the centre might be depicted as being ahead of its time and as becoming vulnerable as a consequence of this.

There is one final element of centre practice that arises from its intention to work and function as a co-operative that is worthy of discussion before this chapter closes, and that relates to leadership and to perceptions by outsiders of whether or not leadership is evident in such a centre in the forms with which they are most familiar. The following letter was sent to the Co-operative Development Worker of the Sheffield Development Co-operative (SDC) by the centre in order to log with the SDC its concerns at how its structures and also key actors within those structures were misunderstood and misrepresented in the 'outside world':

> We wish to log with you our concerns in respect of our provision but also in regard to the co-operative childcare sector itself. It is clear to us that the LA [local authority] misunderstands the concept and workings of co-operatives, and the role of individuals in such co-operatives.
>
> It is something we have raised consistently with Officers of the Council, especially in respect of their previous inspection processes, now transferred to Ofsted and which have been, through Ofsted, so much more developmental and inclusive than those delivered by the City Council which were in our and the community sector's experiences solely delivered on a policing basis to find 'wrong doing'. One consistent focus of this approach by them is finding fault with our co-operative status. The LA is insistent that we put into place the 'normal' hierarchies

to fit into their way of working with identifiable heads. We already have identifiable co-ordinators and leads under a co-operative structure.

In response Ms Meleady had, as you know, agreed to take on this mantle and to be the co-operative's public spokesperson, but we wish to log with you that we are fearful that she may become a target in this regard and we are further fearful of her being victimised as a result given our ongoing history of being outside of the 'norms', i.e. being a co-operative, employing so many men in childcare and also our work and inclusion at all levels, of such high numbers of BME people, combined with the fact that our service challenges institutions on behalf of vulnerable and marginalised individuals and groups in our society.

Whilst we have leading and supporting roles in the co-operative no one in reality is the head or is dominant, it is a collective.

Is there any way that we can raise awareness of co-operatives with them and to dissuade them from these constant misrepresentations of our organisation and the particular individual concerned? Please do not say change the public spokesperson format of House Lead. We have discussed this and whilst Chrissy would no doubt jump at the chance of this happening there is no one else willing or able to carry at this stage such a poisoned chalice.

We are logging our worries with the Sheffield Racial Equality Council also so that there is a paper trail of our concerns if that is alright with you.

The concerns around how co-operatives are perceived were not unfounded, and this extract indicates the steps that such organisations may feel they have to take in order to protect themselves and key individuals from misconceptions about their work within the co-operative framework.

In Chapter 4, we turn the spotlight upon diversity as a central concept, and look at some of the activities and experiences developed for and with children and young people who use the centre. However, our discussion of the centre's relationship with the local authority is not yet complete and we return to this in Chapter 6.

# 4

# DIVERSITY AS A CORNERSTONE OF CENTRE DEVELOPMENT

We believe that children learn best when their self-identity is strong, when they can see that their lifestyle and their family members are valued and when they come to recognise and accept that there are many ways for people to live their lives.

(Meleady and Broadhead, 2002: 14)

The article from which the above quote is taken is entitled 'The norm not the exception'. The title itself is taken from a report produced together by children, parents and workers at the centre. The quote refers, in particular, to a long-standing focus on men's full participation in childcare and early education, briefly referenced in previous chapters and an aspect to be explored further in this chapter, along with others aspects – or facets – of diversity, which also of course encompasses inclusion, multistrand equality and anti-discrimination in all its forms. The title reflects the view that men working with children should be an accepted norm in society; that this is a fundamental entitlement for the children as well as for the men. We have had some references in the narratives previously explored, to the positive role models that men have offered to boys at the centre, some of whom may have had no male role models in their lives up to that point.

## Diversity is a diamond with many facets

Diversity encapsulates socio-economic aspects and political affiliations, faiths and belief forms, age, race, ethnicity and nationality, sexuality, family composition, health status, and physical, emotional and mental abilities. Over the years, the work of the centre across these facets has been integral to the steady growth of its national and international reputation. In this chapter and in the next, we focus on both the work within the centre and on the ways in which this work has linked the centre, both nationally and internationally, to activities, campaigning and to social justice agendas of the wider world, from the streets surrounding the centre in Sheffield to refugee camps and palaces across the world.

Before we put some of that work in context, it seems important to draw attention to the downside of being at the cutting edge of practice in relation to the promotion of diversity on such a scale. Promoting diversity on so many planes, as a fundamental cornerstone of daily practice within and beyond the centre, inevitably means challenging accepted norms in society at some point or another. In placing their collective heads above the parapet through their work and through their expressions of intent and practice, the centre workers know that they risk drawing unwanted attention. They know this from their own experiences, some of which are described here.

One example of this was a particularly intense period in 2005. During the period 4 February 2002 to 13 September 2005, a South Yorkshire Police printout, with associated crime numbers, identified 17 separate acts of criminal intent with Sheffield Children's Centre identified as the 'Scene of Crime'. Six of these were criminal damage to buildings, six were theft or burglary, one was 'arson not endangering life' – the centre was empty – and one was assault of a police officer called to the centre to support staff dealing with a violent parent. Apart from the latter incident, the centre workers believe that the remaining attacks were perpetrated by activists who took exception to their activity and staffing profile, and to their work in the community for disabled and minority ethnic groups. During this period, some workers were being harassed as they came to and went from work, often travelling in pairs or small groups to give mutual support. They were being leafleted with race hate flyers. One male Asian worker accepted an envelope thinking it was a card to find the race hate flyer inside. One disabled worker was subject to vitriolic and deeply frightening harassment as he left the centre, and felt he had to remain absent for several days for his own safety. Although these attacks abated and then disappeared altogether, the insidiousness of them was such that centre workers became fearful of reporting their experiences to the police because they felt that they would be difficult to prove, and they feared further and worse reprisals against them as individuals if they did make reports. Kalilah, who works in the early years base, reflected on why the attacks might be occurring:

> I personally think it's because we have so many different cultures working together and the outside world doesn't maybe agree with it and they want the centre to fail, I don't know, trying to break us as a team. But we get through ... you just come in on Monday and then you pick yourself up and start all over again ... we've got CCTVs now.
>
> (Delgado, 2006: 244)

At different points in time, the children have been cared for by workers with a range of assessed abilities, including learning disabilities. Centre policy recognises that, while workers with disabilities may need special levels of support by colleagues, they nevertheless play a central part in the day-to-day interactions with co-workers, with children, with young people and with parents and carers across the spectrum of physical and mental ability; they are integral to the community because the centre community aims to mirror the world in which the children and young people who use the centre live and grow. All workers have colleague and parent mentors to support them and they in turn support other workers.

Chapter 2 presented an extract from the centre's equal opportunities policy; a small part of that is repeated here to reiterate the fundamental commitment to diversity and the acknowledgement of the associated challenges of such a commitment, even today.

> All children, adults and families, plus communities should have the opportunity to access, take up and receive the services we offer and to achieve just and fair outcomes for themselves, irrespective of their colour, race, nationality, ethnic origin, religion, gender, marital status, sexual orientation, age or disability.
>
> Unfortunately there is evidence to show that individuals are discriminated against in many walks of life. The existence of equality of opportunity cannot be taken for granted.
>
> Organisations must put in place special arrangements to ensure that the users of their services, or members, are treated fairly and in a manner that results in positive outcomes.

In being so explicit in acknowledging its own responsibilities, the centre also opens itself up to exploitation by those who are so inclined; it draws attention, intentionally, to its own potential omissions and weaknesses by saying that all organisations must continually be vigilant in relation to fair treatment of service users and service workers.

Through training and development, and through day-to-day conversations around the topic and around children's cultural entitlements, centre workers become aware of the real dangers in pathologising and stereotyping differences across individuals and groups. They aim to fulfil these aspirations of policy and practice through their curriculum and through the creation of a balanced environment with men and women, gay and straight, with a range of abilities and from a range of ethnic groups representing a range of cultures and traditions, and engaging with children and families who will, variously, also reflect those cultures, traditions and lifestyles. From these shared and multiple perspectives, workers, children and parents come together to co-construct an integrated community in which children and adults grow and learn together, and gradually come to better understand the positive attributes of interconnections between lifestyle choices, personal identity and prevailing norms.

These are not small aspirations and require a deep commitment to such principles over an extended period to bring such challenging policy to life as day-to-day practices, and sometimes, as we have seen above, in the face of local and vitriolic opposition.

It is in this respect perhaps that the centre's approach is most substantially socio-political. It may seem to have nothing in common with childcare and early education, but let us return briefly to Dahlberg and Moss's (2005) work referenced in Chapter 1. They talk of preschools across Europe having 'opened up difference as a subject of minor politics' (2005: 171) and of pre-schools being 'sites for democratic practice'. They identify the construct of the 'experimenting pedagogue' within the 'experimenting preschool' and an 'experimenting local community' (2005: 185) ultimately aligning these with the *'experimenting state'*. They locate these interrelated constructs within a *'utopian state'*; a sense of what might emerge and what might fundamentally change for the better through truly embracing diversity, in the way societies live and work and interconnect. There are parallels here with the development of Sheffield Children's Centre from its days as childcare provider in a community programme located in a church hall. Over its years of development, the centre's ethos has progressed through these 'experimental' phases as it has framed, filled out and deepened its policies and practices around the facets of diversity – as it has gradually 'cut and polished the diamond' to reveal the glow beneath. In relation to Dahlberg and Moss's analogy above, the centre should therefore have real potential to subsequently influence the wider work of the state, given the state's current commitment to combating disadvantage and to ensuring that *Every Child Matters* (DfES, 2003) brings about the required changes to and integration of services for children and families, and that these developments retain the close and active involvement of the wider community.

Centre practices have challenged accepted norms, not only through a policy of including 50 per cent men in the workforce (paid and unpaid), but also, for example, as we saw in the previous chapter, through locating children with adults in spaces not traditionally deemed to be 'educational' by 'Under Eights Officers'. Experimenting with the perceived social order brings risk; change brings risk, and an extensive confrontation of accepted norms brings extensive risk. Insider and outsider perspectives might clash in the first instance and it might be only with the passage of time, as the glow emerges, that those who felt threatened by these new perspectives can eventually come to understand them a little better.

The remaining sections of this chapter aim to bring a little of the cutting and polishing alive through a focus on a range of initiatives and activities that have developed in the centre, over time. We'll begin with its local, national and international work with men in childcare, move on to some aspects of its local community work, and finish with the children and with some aspects of the curriculum as manifest through the centre's practices, locally and nationally.

## A focus on men in childcare

Jim's story was elicited through the questionnaire to parents and carers; he responded as a gay father. His response has been extended with italics to bring meaning and continuity to his story as an introduction to this focus on men in childcare.

'*We were* offered positive role models of gay fathers and same-sex households and *this has* helped both my children to value our family, and has made parenting them so much easier. They [the centre] have supported my family and helped our children to be open about their lives.

'Other gay men and lesbians use the centre and recommended it. The gay fathers' group offers practical, moral and social support to our children and to us, as fathers. Prejudice is always there, especially towards gay fathers, and the centre mitigates this.

'We know of very few places that support diversity in the city; we've never thought of our life other than with the centre.

'*It would be helpful if* more literature *was* produced, targeted towards same-sex relationships and families in the past.

'We've learned parenting skills through workshops and child development needs through seminars and help at the centre. We've also learnt as a family to speak Spanish from attending family language workshops.'

Jim portrays his own and his children's experiences as rich and varied, where his sexuality is respected but not highlighted, and his shared experiences with his children both support and inform them all, in the company of others. It is also worth noting that bisexual and trans families also use the centre and are employed in the centre, as are gay and lesbian workers ('trans' transsexual, transgender, and so on).

Peter's reflections in Delgado's work (2006: 233) not only illustrate a dimension of men's involvement in the centre but also show, as many of the testimonies in Chapter 1 did, how individuals progress, in this case, from service user as a child, to centre worker, combining work with study and gaining job satisfaction along the way:

I used to come here as a kid, to the out-of-school service. My sister, who is nine, used to come here to the baby room and to bases one and two. One of my best mates, his mom works here. So we just came here after school and kind of, it's always been here for years, so it's something I just felt natural doing. The first day I worked here, I really enjoyed it because the kids, they make me feel good, I just like it very much. I only come here about three days a week now. But first it was more and they made me feel good, they made me feel like, a little younger and gave me some energy back or something like that. And it was so much better because before I was working at D's Pizza and that was a boring part-time job. I worked at nights. Now I work in the daytime. I can still do school and can have like a social life in the evening so it's the best job, the best part-time job I could find.

At the turn of this century, the government made an explicit commitment to raising the numbers of men working in the early education and childcare sectors. A target of 6 per cent was set for Early Years Development and Childcare Partnerships. These EYDCPs were new local authority committees tasked with developing integrated services for children and families, the precursor of the integrated Children's Services now manifest in local authorities through the Children Act 2004. The EYDCPs worked towards the bringing together of the, previously separately evolving, maintained, private- and voluntary-sector providers of care and education for young children and services for families through the integration, across every local authority, of the health, education and social policy sectors. Despite this target-setting of 6 per cent, by June 2005, only 2 per cent of the overall workforce was male (Clemens *et al.*, 2005).

Owen (2003: 100) points out that changing the gender mix requires an understanding of why childcare work is as gendered as it is, stating, 'When men enter this most archetypal female occupation, their motives may be thought suspect and their sexuality called into question.' There is one further aspect of legislation relating to sexuality, and with particular implications for male workers, that centre workers feel strongly has had a long-standing and detrimental impact on society's willingness to accept men, especially gay men, as workers with children.

The Local Government Act 1988, in Section 28, stated that a local authority was not permitted to 'intentionally promote homosexuality' or to promote the teaching in any maintained school of 'the acceptability of homosexuality as a pretended family relationship'. This act remained in force in England until 2003 and in Scotland until 2000, and virtually stifled national debates around the role of men and, in particular, the role of gay men in work with children. Schools became afraid to speak about family lifestyles that included homosexuality; teachers became afraid to challenge homophobic behaviour in case this was seen as 'promoting homosexuality', and were also afraid to answer questions from children and young people around homosexuality. In educational contexts, gay lifestyles went underground to a large extent during this period – the very period when the centre was promoting acceptance of diverse lifestyles as a fundamental right of all: staff, parents, carers, children and young people. Once again, it was swimming against the tide in its work and policy development, while also being a precursor to future government policy.

As Maggie remarked when reflecting on this era: 'You take a stand and pressure is put on everyone.' She recalled a time during this period when local authority personnel had put pressure on the centre to get rid of male workers because of unfounded and very general concerns about 'abuse'. Centre workers saw this as an unacceptable level of hysteria born of ignorance rather than concern for children. Maggie also recalled a situation during this period when a lesbian couple specifically requested that their children did not have contact with male staff members. Maggie recalls that one of the lesbian parents asked, 'Is he a puff?' In the early days and on into the turn of the century, male staff would have to go 'over and above', as Maggie described it, to be accepted by the mainstream and also by their female colleagues in the centre. One Asian male staff worker talked of the rejection he experienced from his own community for his choice of work. Confronting stereotypes is never going to be easy.

There had been a situation, long before the designation of the centre as an EEC when a parent had accused a male staff member of abuse of her child in the centre. Prior to becoming the EEC evaluator, PB had offered some development sessions to staff. One of these, focusing on curriculum development, had changed focus when one of the male workers had left the session in tears, and the remaining workers had explained his current circumstances to PB. He returned to the session, but the focus was shifted, and from these discussions subsequently emerged a detailed policy document for child protection that became an influential document for other providers over time. Centre workers became trainers for other providers and several local authorities in terms of wider policy development in this area. The policy related both to the protection of children through standard practices as applicable to all workers – male and female – and to the protection of staff from unfounded accusations by parents. The male worker was subsequently exonerated after investigation but the case had a long-term and detrimental impact on him, and inevitably reverberated around and beyond the centre for some time. Another worker remarked in the questionnaires undertaken for the EEC work, several years later, 'Male workers are vulnerable and need to be aware of the possibility of allegations.' The centre, in recognising and addressing this, has given a lead to other providers in the sector, always taking as its starting point a view that protecting children should have no gender bias.

Within the questionnaires, workers had recognised the longer-term and positive impact of employing men, commenting as follows: 'Mothers come to acknowledge the role men can play when there are positive responses from their own children' and 'Lone fathers bring their children because of the men.'

This last quote suggests that the traditional feminising of childcare was being positively addressed in the centre as men, both workers and parents, came to feel more comfortable in this space, over time. However, being at the cutting edge in this way also brings new responsibilities for the male workers, as this one remarked in his questionnaire: 'I am more conscious of the responsibility on us at the centre to set a good and constant example to others because of the discrimination.'

Female workers at the centre shared their own changing attitudes to men in the workplace. One wrote:

I've seen it bring out the gentle side in men. I've seen that men do need to take responsibility for shaping children's attitudes to them. I understand now that men can work just as well as women with children.

Experience changes perceptions, and this in turn brings about key shifts in cultural norms. This is the case for workers at the centre, as well as for wider society, and is something the centre must actively engage with if perspectives are to shift.

Children and young people in the holiday club also brought some interesting insights to this focus on men in childcare. To facilitate some focus group work with mixed age groups, the children and young people were given some statements to consider and then asked to consider whether each was true or false. They were also invited to share other comments with PB, who was facilitating these discussions. More than anything, their reflections illustrated their perceived need for balance in the workforce, being central to a balanced curriculum, although they did not couch their comments in such terms. They talked practically and eloquently about their personal experiences of having men and women around them on a regular basis, and about men's and women's attitudes to childcare and to life more generally. As would be the case with any group of adults, these children's reflections varied, influenced undoubtedly by their own experiences and by the attitudes of a wide range of associated adults.

Five of the statements, and their associated true (T) false (F) responses and additional comments are shared here.

### Statement 1: It's usually women that look after children: – 13T, 4F, 1DK (don't know)

The following are additional comments taken from the subsequent discussion (individual comments are separated by a semi-colon).

If you're in danger men look after you; there's no difference between men and women; men and women equally look after children; they both try their hardest; women stay with you, men leave; more women think children are cute; men think it's a girl thing.

### Statement 2: Most men don't want jobs looking after children: – 7T, 9F, 2DK

A few men want to but most men don't; men enjoy looking after you; my dad looks after me every day; men look after you by shouting, then they laugh; if mum goes out, dad looks after you; sometimes dad relaxes, sometimes he plays but even when he's not playing he's looking after me; they think it's sissy; people don't remember what it's like being a child; they think children are annoying; they think it's a boring job; they think it's a woman's job; they think it's not an important job.

### Statement 3: Women like you to be quiet but men let you be noisy: – 8T, 8F, 2DK

Men let you have fun; I know some men and some women like that; they treat you the same; mum lets me stay up and dad makes me go to bed; when dad plays guitar mum makes him stop.

### Statement 4: Men are more fun when you're playing than women are: – 7T, 7F, 4DK

Men take us somewhere and women just have coffee; *boy* – men always play with you, *girl replies* – it never happens to me; they can both be fun; dad puts his feet up mum doesn't; dad watches TV; women just say sit down.

### Statement 5: I like being looked after by men and women at the Children's Centre: – 15T, 3F

They treat you the same; they do different activities; if you just have men it's all boys things and if you have both it's mixed; they have different opinions; I'd rather have women; I'd rather have men 'cos they're nicer, they wear nice clothes; women do more things, help you and play games; men chase you and are funny; women mop the floor and men work; if somebody says something you're not interested in you can talk to other people, there's more likely to be people interested in what you're interested in.

These statements and discussions have contributed to national conferences on men in childcare, some in collaboration with the local authority, and international conferences in Ireland, Scotland, Europe and the USA. Many visitors have attended the centre to talk to workers about these issues, and centre workers, both male and female, have become involved in local and national cases supporting and advising men who have been falsely accused of child abuse in the workplace. The centre's work in relation to men in child-care has brought it into conflict with feminist groups, and it has become expert in defending its policies and practices and debating the issues. Its work in establishing fathers' groups, gay fathers' groups and lesbian mothers' groups has had national spin-offs, with other service providers coming to the centre for insights and ways forward in their own provision. The emphasis has been on creating a male- and father-friendly inclusive environment. This includes support for adolescent fathers and older fathers, facilitating contacts between children and their non-resident fathers, grandfathers' groups, fathers in prison and pre-natal and parenting groups to enhance fatherhood skills and emotional intelligence, and specific support for disabled fathers and for fathers across a wide range of cultural groups. The list could go on. The underpinning principle of this and other work at the centre has always been to support the wider reconstruction of family life in society by driving back restrictive norms.

## Working with the wider community

Not all of these activities will necessarily be seen as innovative. Many of them may now be available in similar forms in Children's Centres across the country. However, in giving as complete a picture as possible of the innovative work of the centre in establishing such services when they were less prevalent, we also aim to illustrate the extent of its commitment to diversity as an underlying premise. Our aim is also to illustrate that the curriculum is conceived of as not only the educational experiences of children (although these are central) but that the children's experiences are enmeshed within strands of related activities for family and community. Children's learning is important but is just a part of the wider 'curriculum' on offer at the centre.

### Intergenerational activity

The workers developed links with a lunch club and associated daycare service in an adjacent community centre where provision was being made for senior citizens. The children visit the lunch club, and vice versa, to establish inter-generational links for both the young and old, many of whom may not have such links within their own family structures.

Intergenerational mentoring is ongoing, although seldom explicitly evi-dent in day-to-day activities. Older adults may mentor young people; the centre makes provision, occasionally, for young people who have been excluded from school, and their day-to-day relationships with older adults – involved as unpaid workers – can have a calming influence. Crochet lessons have been provided for younger members of the out-of-school club by older community members, and old songs taught, sometimes in languages other than English. In these and other activities, minority ethnic adults contribute to the awareness of other cultural identities. Older people have supported children's and young people's reading development and have also taught sign language. Male elders have mentored, unrelated, lone-parent fathers and adolescent fathers. Female elders help younger mothers, some of whom are no longer in contact with their own families, perhaps because of their own pregnancy, and some of whom have been in care and may not have seen any member of their birth family for a long period. When young people with young parents have had problems at school, centre workers have come to realise that situations become more facilitative if a community elder visits the school with the young person and her/his young parent. They have found that teachers and senior staff in schools, and local authority staff, have responded differently in the presence of a mature adult. A mentor, operating in this way, is able to prepare the family for the forthcoming interaction, to support them during the interaction and to try to ensure that the discussion does not become confrontational through tension and anxiety.

Through engaging with elders in the community, centre workers have come to better understand what older people have to offer, how skilful and knowledgeable they can be, but also how the elders come to believe that a local community feels that they have nothing to offer. The workers also began to understand, through ongoing dialogues, that older people had safety issues in their community, often associated with groups of teenagers 'out and about'. Working together helped alleviate these fears for elders, and to sensitise young people to the potential vulnerability of the older members of the community. Centre workers came to believe that it is good for children and young people to see older people in employment and volunteering in unpaid work.

Sometimes the young mentor the older community members in the out-of-school clubs where the young demonstrate the use of computers and mobile phones. Conversations can also alert older members of the community to the fears and isolation of younger members.

The centre has supported children with terminal illnesses and their families. Hanging in the workers' restroom is a foot imprint from Ayesha, who died when six months old. The family also have an imprint of Ayesha's foot, and centre workers are happy to remember and celebrate her brief life and the part that they played in supporting Ayesha and her family.

### The Female Genital Mutilation Group

The centre has supported this group of women over an extended period. The group grew, slowly but steadily, from one woman who had gained the courage to talk to a worker, with whom she culturally identified, about her personal circumstances in relation to female genital mutilation, and the physical difficulties she was experiencing as a result of this. Gradually the workers became aware that there were other women experiencing similar difficulties in the local community and, equally gradually, through word of mouth, women began to accept that the centre was somewhere they could come, in confidence, to get emotional and medical support for their circumstances. As in other areas, this has spearheaded related national activities in the dissemination of this very sensitive area of work.

As the group grew, over time, the focus of meetings was on self-care and social activities. Centre workers sought opportunities to raise awareness, with the women, about the oppression associated with these long-standing practices within their own culture. However, these discussions always had to be sensitively undertaken as women might leave the centre and its support if they felt themselves to be placed in untenable positions in relation to long-standing cultural practices and norms within their own communities. There was considerable consternation among group members when the local authority began issuing letters stating that it was illegal for parents to take daughters back to their own countries for circumcision and then return to the UK. Centre workers faced huge personal dilemmas in wanting to remain in contact with the women and yet also wanting to prevent the female cutting taking place for the next generation of girls. Here, respect for cultural norms and for lifestyle choices, as a fundamental tenet of practice, is put to its most arduous test for the workers. However, they maintained, in being true to their own principles of practice, that deep and abiding cultural change would not come through imposition but through discussion of traditions and concerns in trustful partnerships. The changes, they believed, would have to come from the women themselves acting to alter the cultural norms and values within their own communities.

Clearly these are not easy decisions to take in these circumstances, but they are the kinds of decisions and approaches that have to be made and acted upon if a service describes itself as responsive to local community needs. Those needs will inevitably manifest themselves in different, and sometimes difficult, ways.

### The Fit Kids Club and mental health support

The centre has operated a Fit Kids initiative for many years. These sessions within nursery and within the out-of-school and holiday clubs incorporate teamwork through vigorous and culturally diverse team games. The club promotes fitness in the most diverse of ways and is not only a focus on exercise. A wide range of bodily images are presented and discussed with children and young people, cookery sessions from all cultures are undertaken, there are shopping expeditions for small groups of young people to reflect their ethnic identity or the multiple cultural identities that they may be choosing to adopt. Centre workers arrange visits to or from hairdressers, and make-up advice, again to reflect the multiple ethnic identities present in the centre (both workers and service users), and also visits to and with personal trainers. They have developed links with the local, national football team.

The aim is also to increase body understanding and awareness, and to broaden personal knowledge in relation to nutrition and health. Many of the activities are informative and helpful for workers as well as for children, young people and parents/carers; everyone is equal in their learning experiences and enjoyment. A teenager with facial scarring and a young child with hair loss from chemotherapy are just two who have been helped through these ongoing activities and facilities.

It is within this broader context that mental health issues are also addressed, and benefit both centre users and the wider community. Counselling services with different forms of psychotherapy are offered. Many services are offered by qualified volunteers, as we saw from the wide team of workers involved in earlier chapters. These links with volunteers create closer working partnerships between the centre and other community services but, as we have also seen in previous chapters, these partnerships emerge through '*osmosis' premised on equity*' rather than through '*strategic planning to targets*'. The professional volunteers hear about and are attracted to the ethos of the centre; sometimes being actively recruited. This wider impact is integral to the centre's *heartland*, just as the centre's capacity to engage with women who have been circumcised, and with older and younger members of the community, is also integral to its '*heartland*'. We will return to this discussion in the closing chapter of the book.

Centre workers act as translators and intermediaries in supporting access to all services, and in working to ensure that the services are culturally appropriate – in cases, for example, where women prefer to be seen by professional women. The wide cultural experiences of staff have enabled them to raise awareness of cultural norms in local hospitals, doctors' surgeries and schools, where their advice is often sought in relation to individual cases presenting; they also, as we have noted, attend these services with parents and carers.

## A focus on children's learning

This section opens with a reflection from Kalilah, a key worker at the centre, who believes that due attention must be given to children's emotional needs in order to support them in being best placed to access their curricular experiences:

> The time that the child is with you, from 8 'til 6, you try and fill that gap in their lives and you make them feel that they're the most important people and that they deserve all the love and care. And that's what we're here to give them. And that's where the one-to-one contact comes in ... it's just trying to build on their lives and making them feel they are wanted, that we love them and that we're here for them.

Jenny, one of the long-standing workers from whom we have heard in previous chapters, has lead responsibility for curriculum training and development for the paid and unpaid workers. Put simply in her words, 'I'm involved in decisions relating to training and staffing. I cover the curriculum alongside the staff. We each have something different to give: culture, language, interests.'

The workers do recognise some tensions in relation to a centrally determined curriculum in that they do not feel that it takes sufficient account of individual children's cultural experiences within and beyond their setting, nor of the aspirations that workers ascribe as being fundamental to their own provision in terms of how they interpret equality of opportunity. They see a tension around a given curriculum because they believe that it can deny choice and identity to the child – in discussions they have expressed a view that the given curriculum is more concerned with assimilation and compliance rather than being about identity, choice and decision-making by the child.

In one of the many discussions that supported the writing of this book, Maggie reflected that, in her view, other centres may promote an ideal of childhood that aims to protect children who experience difficulties in their lives from the experiences that are perceived as 'bad'. At the centre, workers aim to actively engage with a view that such experiences are integral to the child's experience and should not be denied or avoided or labelled. Maggie felt that it was to do the child a disservice if the curriculum were such that it idealised childhood and denied the voice and experience of reality as lived in their day-to-day lives. This was not to suggest that Maggie was maintaining that a curriculum should be premised on 'bad' experiences, but rather that they should not be overlooked by adults responding to children as they engaged with the learning environment. It's an integral part of seeing and of working with the whole child. Such a fundamental approach requires considerable sensitivity on the part of the adults, of course.

Our discussion at this time progressed to the notion of 'oasis' or to what Maggie also termed 'the Habitat nurseries', something she had also reflected on in Delgado's work (2006: 219):

> Poverty is a big issue. Making a nice environment in the nursery is not enough – and this is not to disrespect the nice nurseries. You go to the beautiful and gorgeous places and see that the nursery is an oasis for the children. It doesn't matter what happens outside, at home or in the community as long as we provide them with a nice little environment, use the equipment and have a nice time with the staff there. But if they go back home and that home has been burnt down because they are Pakistanis or if the mother is mentally ill and she can't cook dinner that doesn't bother us because we are in the oasis. That is an alien concept to us. We try to think that we can do something for the whole of the child's life. That is what we are looking at ... There is no point in a child coming here and after a couple of hours of niceness go home to poverty and be picked on for race, because his mum is a lesbian or his dad is gay or whatever. We have to look at and work with families to do the best for all ...

She felt that, often, such sites were more attuned to adults' sensitivities (and to women's sensitivities) than to children's. Exotic artefacts might be brought in that looked attractive but had no meaning in the child's own life; sometimes, the curriculum was perceived by adults as cultural compensation when in fact the providing adults, because of their own cultural ignorance, had no sense of any cultural richness in the child's own life outside of their nursery. The 'oasis' preserved a lack of typicality in the child's life in that it could exist as it did only if it could keep the encroaching surroundings of the wider community at bay in some way.

In moving the discussion forward, and in seeking to illustrate innovative practice in curriculum development, let us examine one particular experience established for children and young people at the centre during the 1990s. This seems a more useful way of illustrating the centre's perspective on curriculum as arising from the children's needs and interests rather than, predominantly, from the adults' agenda or from a government agenda within a policy context that has no link to the children's and young people's day-to-day lives as lived in the centre and the wider community.

## The Shack

For many years, the centre had supported the children and young people who used the services through the Children's Council. In this forum, the children and young people aged from 5 to 16 years made decisions that informed the activities provided for them and with them in the out-of-school and holiday clubs. During the early 1990s, the Children's Council discussed a report, 'Children as community leaders: a programme for democratic inclusion in decision-making'. The children decided that their childhood culture was being ignored, a criticism both of the centre and of the wider community. If we give voice to children and young people we must be prepared for their criticisms. The council decided that they wished to establish an international centre for childhood culture and the arts. Jenny assisted them with some funding from the centre's income, and adults and children also fundraised. Over time, artists from other countries were invited to share their work with the children, as well as with workers and parents – indeed with all who were interested – and workers also visited other countries to develop their own body of knowledge about international arts and culture. The Shack, still at the conceptual stage, evolved from the children's work with artists, and the children and young people developed the name. At this point, the Shack was a conceptual space owned by children and young people, and facilitated by adults in close discussion with the Children's Council.

As this initiative progressed, the requirements for children's participation in local decision-making were also gaining momentum, as has been discussed in Chapter 2. The children and young people began to focus on and develop their ideas about and understanding of children's rights, and also became interested in extending their experiences of arts and crafts. Their work and focus linked them with the Ark in Dublin and with the Metropolis in Amsterdam, and visits were made.

As the initiative gathered momentum, the children, adults and young people began negotiations to become part of the millennium developments in the city. They found money for a business plan built around the Shack and children as community leaders. However, they then found themselves in competition with another initiative being developed by the City Council. Centre workers believed that their own initiative was most strongly rooted in children's ideas and actions, but they were not successful in gaining the necessary funding for moving the Shack from a virtual space to a real space. The associated activities and ideas still remain integral to the centre's work, as the next section shows.

## The use of film

With financial support from fundraising, the children and young people purchased film production equipment and began to develop their understanding of the power of the media, as well as their expertise in the use of technology. Students from the Media School at the nearby college came in to help on a regular basis.

Children who were terminally ill used the equipment to leave personal legacies for their friends and family by creating personal diaries. In this way, they prepared themselves for death, and their friends and family for bereavement. Children going for adoption made videos of their past lives as testimony for themselves and as shared autobiography for their new families. Centre workers began to realise that young children could become technical experts, and also recognised the liberating experience that media technology provided for children who were having difficulties in developing their literacy skills. Children began to record stories and film of their grandparents and through this could engage in discussion with centre workers about death and bereavement as a normal aspect of the life cycle. They recorded songs. They made a film about road safety and keeping safe in fires. Sheffield Independent Television helped in professionalising the films, also working with the children and young people. Some of the young people attending the out-of-school service had been temporarily excluded from school for their behaviour. They made a video about bullying and disaffection. With support, they addressed issues around racial tension born of their own school experiences. They also addressed issues around dual heritage, exploring their own feelings and experiences, and using these as a basis for raising awareness more widely and for stimulating discussion about issues seldom discussed in the public domain.

The children and young people showed their films at the nearby independent cinema, and this gave credibility and validity to their work. Some films were translated so that the children could show them at home. Parents were able to take the cameras home to make short films to be shown at the centre and borrowed by other children and young people. These then promoted multilingual practices and cultural understanding; they vividly illustrated alternative lifestyles, forging new ways of living and working together. One white British mother remarked to workers, 'My daughter loves Shanaz [centre worker] and wants to dress like her.'

The children loaned the equipment, for payment, to older members of the community who wanted to make a film about getting a better deal for older people. They made films about personal struggles and, in better understanding their past, they shaped their futures, driven by an agenda of dignity and pride and not by a government agenda designed to reach targets.

Giving voice to children and young people in this way requires workers to be creative and energetic. Empowering them in this way also requires the setting of limits and boundaries, and these have to be negotiated and rene-gotiated constantly. Children and young people will inevitably challenge boundaries, and balance has to be discovered for everyone, in order to keep up the momentum of the working partnerships; respect will not be won by being dictatorial. But the workers began to see how previously disaffected children and young people could begin to take responsibility and to gradually recognise the impact they can have, through active participation, in their own communities. They saw the young people begin to conceive of them-selves as contributors to the social good. A group of young people met with a local politician, who remarked upon the incisive questions that they asked in the meeting. Children and young people came to see and understand their role as citizens.

Through activities of this kind, the curriculum becomes an extension of everyday life, children help to build the curriculum with their own cultural background, and then surprise adults with their knowledge and under-standing, taking the curriculum further than conceived of by adults. The curriculum, lived in this way, is inherently anti-discriminatory as it values and includes all, and is actively used to challenge racism, discrimination and other forms of oppression. The curriculum is the equal opportunities policy in action, going far beyond the promotion of acceptance and tolerance, and seeking to shift mainstream relationships. We can see why this might bring the centre into conflict with others who seek, for their own reasons, to pre-vent such messages reaching the public domain and why the experiences of centre workers can be so negative and frightening at times as the workers and service users together begin to seek paradigms of truth that go beyond mainstream value systems. Centre workers believe that they have enhanced the vision of how other institutions maintain discriminatory practices.

The history and development of the centre is closely aligned with the problems of its participants, of adults – service providers and service users – and of children and young people. Not all of the initiatives described in Chapter 4 happened at once, but they are linked by biographical events in the lives of adults and children. Not everyone feels comfortable in such an environment, for a range of reasons and sometimes because they do not wish to confront the realities of their own experiences and legacies.

The centre takes guidance for its work and for its curriculum development from religious groups in the community; the workers also seek spiritual gui-dance for their work in relation to the multiple religions that are manifest in their curricular activities. They see spirituality as an integral part of child protection and of the maintaining of a sense of connectedness across the multiple faiths and cultures that are reflected in the ongoing work. They use history, oral traditions and life stories to bring their curriculum alive, to root the curriculum and related experiences in a sense of self and of personal identity. They aim to bring meaning to the following:

> Communities, like individual human beings, bring to the process of constructing their own futures certain cultural and social characteristics of an organic nature. A community, to develop, must also initiate,

explore options, and learn by trial and error. It needs space to do that. Moreover, institutions in the larger environment, with whom communities interact, must recognise that individual communities are different and they change over time . . .

(Myers, 1992: 317)

There are two key elements to Myers' words that would influence and even determine the future of the centre as time unfolded: the extent to which it might be allowed to learn from trial and error and the extent to which a powerful, mainstream institution in the wider environment, in this case the local authority, could recognise and accept the socio-cultural and socio-political contributions of Sheffield Children's Centre as a community provider. The final chapter returns to this discussion. Prior to that, Chapter 5 puts a little more flesh on the international bones of the centre's work.

# 5

# INTERNATIONAL NETWORKS AND GLOBAL JUSTICE: A RECIPROCAL HIGHWAY FOR ONGOING EVOLUTION

Previous chapters have sought to describe, to evidence and to develop a picture of the centre's work within both a socio-cultural and a socio-political paradigm, and to embed these paradigms within a wider view of the centre as developing a project identity. The descriptions and narratives have been built around the central constructs of a *reciprocal heartland* and a *catalyst for change* in depicting both the work of and the impact of the centre in creating and sustaining its project identity and, through this, in changing lives and life chances for workers and for community members, adults, children and young people.

The centre has been described as an example of 'a site for democratic practice and minor politics' (Dahlberg and Moss, 2005: 15). These authors describe minor politics as one way in which the nation state and democracy are moved in new directions 'towards wider participation in more negotiations about more issues' (2005: 15). In this chapter, we look beyond the national scene to explore the international work of the Sheffield Children's Centre and consider its potential as a site for democratic practice and minor politics in these arenas also.

A related construct that it seems timely to draw upon at this point, before beginning the more detailed discussion of the centre's international work, is that of *social capital* (Bourdieu, 1986). Gilchrist (2004: 12) talks of social capital as a 'useful way of thinking about community cohesion in terms of the connections and associations that exist between people, groups and communities. Social capital consists of networks and norms operating in civil society.' Baker *et al.* (2004: 36) describe social capital similarly as 'the durable networks of social relationships to which people have access'. They go on to connect *social capital* with *cultural capital*, which they describe as including both people's embodied knowledge and abilities, and their educational credentials. When social capital and cultural capital come together, then, the potential for societal change is enhanced in ways that reflect the use and application of that capital. These constructs have a direct relationship with the establishing of a *project identity* at the centre. An emerging project attracts those with similar aspirations and begins to incrementally build a critical mass of influence and impact. As previous chapters have sought to illustrate, this is done through affirmative action and reaction, through struggle and, we would argue, also through collaborative resistance to prevailing norms and expectations when these are at odds with the aspirational driving force of the project at work.

Drawing on the work of Calhoun (1994) and Castells (2004), Delgado (2006: 207) discusses how ordinary people influence global structures and, within this, how the emergence of a project like the Sheffield Children's Centre 'can be described as a period of resistance identity'. The resistance is a resistance to domination by potentially stronger and more established influences, and by mainstream organisations that do not hold priorities, aims or goals in common with the resisting organisation. It was, as we have seen from previous chapters, in the centre's earliest manifestation, a resistance to perceived cultural inappropriateness in local services that became its earliest driver. It is within these contexts of resistance and alternative ways of being that the centre's social and cultural capital comes into play and subsequently supports it in making a transformation from its period of *resistance identity* into a *project identity* with an inherently greater potential for influencing social change and challenging cultural norms (Delgado, 2006).

Gilchrist (2004: 12), drawing on Woolcock (2001), uses the terms 'bonding, bridging and linking' to explore the application of social capital and goes on to say:

> Bonding capital is made up of the ties between people who are alike or who share a common experience, such as between family and friends. Bridging capital arises from the connections between groups of dissimilar people, such as the different ethnic communities living in the same neighbourhood. Linking capital is used to mediate between different sectors and levels of society, for example between local government and community organisations.

It might be claimed then, on the basis of evidence presented so far, that Sheffield Children's Centre, in a local and national context, is a site where both bonding and bridging capital are strongly manifest. Linking capital has been very evident at a national level in its designation as an Early Excellence Centre; it has been a greater challenge for it at a local level, and here its relationship with the local authority has moved through different phases over the years. Some of this is examined in the final chapter. As far as the centre's international work is concerned we see bonding, bridging and linking capital in evidence, having developed over the years as the work has unfolded and evolved.

In extending the centre's service provision principles internationally, the centre workers drew from the same philosophical well-spring as that which had driven their UK-based work. (There have been many service development activities outside Sheffield, undertaken by centre workers, that space has not permitted us to include in this book.) As we aim to illustrate, the decision to work abroad emerged as naturally from the centre's day-to-day activities as had other aspects of service development. It is perhaps true to say that, as it began its initiatives abroad, the centre workers were unlikely to be thinking of this work in terms of its potential to feed back into the centre's *project identity* – to become the *reciprocal highway for ongoing evolution* of this chapter's title. They were more likely to be responding, as before, to perceived need in communities with whom they already identified for a wide range of reasons, and in whom they recognised a marginalised status that could be improved with affirmative action. In Gilchrist's statement above, bridging capital extends to 'dissimilar people in the same neighbourhood' but, for centre workers, 'neighbourhood' has always been a relative term that knows no geographical boundaries. In drawing on principles of social justice and parity as underpinning constructs for their work, it might seem almost natural that it would extend to global locations; a form of natural growth was occurring, a growth that would extend their social and cultural capital incrementally.

The principles for the co-operative work, nationally and internationally, have much in common and relate to the need for redistribution of resources and of wealth, power and skills both within and between countries. We might conceive of the centre's work as aiming to contribute to the development of a participatory democracy in political, economic and social contexts, one that includes marginalised people. In its work, the centre is looking for alternative processes of participation and an alternative way of creating, sustaining and regenerating democratic institutions. Underpinning these principles is an ideology that draws from a recognised need to understand the inequalities, discriminations and structural problems that create injustice and suffering both at home and globally. The emphasis, nationally and internationally, has always been upon the development of practical community alternatives so people could see an immediate improvement in their circumstances. Both nationally and internationally, this has always included lobbying and advocacy, the building and maintenance of links and networks, and a calling for greater accountability and transparency from local and national governments. It has also called for team working between community members and support workers.

The previous chapters have sought to illustrate these principles and their underpinning ideology in a national context. This chapter now builds on this with global perspectives.

## Working in Ethiopia

The centre's work in Ethiopia began in the early 1980s with a direct request from communities living in the Mekelle area of Ethiopia in the state of Tigray. Centre workers had worked closely with different members and families of the Ethiopian and Eritrean communities in South Yorkshire, many of whom had fled from the Derg regime in Ethiopia. Much of this local work had been in the form of advocacy for ascribing refugee status to individuals and in offering free childcare provision for parents and carers as families sought to establish themselves within the local community.

Almost all of the adults and children who came into the orbit of the centre had suffered trauma from their experiences both within Ethiopia and in their travels to what they hoped would be safety. Centre workers provided support. Subsequently, it was word of mouth to family members still in Ethiopia from their relatives in Sheffield that led to the request for support for families still in Ethiopia, as the early impact of famine started to take hold. Families in South Yorkshire were trying to send aid to relatives in Ethiopia and they were starting to realise that this was not getting through. Also, some families in South Yorkshire were trying to reunite with close family members who had been left behind and whose lives were at risk.

Centre staff began to forge links with embassies in contact with the Derg and also, as their activities progressed and gained momentum, contacted other national and international aid agencies, seeking ways to work with them and to develop their own understandings within the centre of how to undertake work of this kind most effectively. These links allowed them to begin to facilitate access to routes and means of transferring aid from families in South Yorkshire to family members still in Ethiopia. The centre began to highlight and promote the issues and became involved in developing and co-ordinating a famine relief group within South Yorkshire. This included Ethiopian parents working alongside centre workers and legal service workers acting voluntarily in support of the emerging initiatives.

The centre continued to provide aid to provisions in the Mekelle area, particularly round the area of Maichew, one of the worst-hit areas of famine. They facilitated the allocation of medical staff to assist; nurses went over as volunteers. Some of these were individuals who had already established links with the centre and there were also trainee nurses involved. The trainee nurses were training in local colleges with which the centre had close links, and were gaining valuable overseas experience from their volunteering.

Centre workers visited the area to assess the situation. Some also relocated there for extended periods to support the ongoing development work in relation to famine relief and the development of services for children and families, such as childcare services. Individuals have come over to the centre from Ethiopia to connect with the centre, to gain experience of centre-based working and to gain qualifications, and then to return to Ethiopia to continue the work. A mentoring support service for these Ethiopian workers was subsequently established though email and telephone links.

In the development of community services, culturally appropriate play resources have been made available for the local children. Local people have been employed to produce these resources; this develops local employment opportunities. Medical aid has been provided from local hospitals in South Yorkshire with resources from hospital closures being bought at auction. Liaison with medical companies brought donations of medicine, and the centre became involved in networks that were working closely with hospital and medical staff in Mekelle. In March 2007, the centre liaised with a health visitor and a social worker who, in keeping with ongoing practice, paid for themselves to go across to Ethiopia. They each took leave of absence from their own jobs for a month so as to support the development of the work there, and also to gain valuable professional development experience.

The centre worked with Sheffield Health Action Resource for Ethiopia (SHARE). This action group was formed by the Friends of Ethiopia in the UK, of which Sheffield Children's Centre was a member. The group's main aim was to establish a modest collaborative link between Central Sheffield Hospitals and Mekelle Hospital in the state of Tigray, northern Ethiopia.

Part of the way in which the work of the centre builds social capital is illustrated in the stories of Solomon and Ben. These are two young men who have attended the centre from the age of 6 months. Solomon's ethnicity is black Ethiopian, white British. Ben is white British. As young adolescents, involved with the out-of-school club, they became involved in fundraising for the relief work in Ethiopia. In their late teens, and aware of the ongoing work in Ethiopia through discussions with workers and volunteers, the two boys decided that they wanted to go across to work in a Mekelle kindergarten with which the centre had established links. Solomon and Ben did this in their gap year. They took resources with them bought with funds raised from the local community. Several years later, Solomon reflected on this work as follows:

> It was a life-changing experience. We have so much in the West yet they have so little, and yet what little they have, they are grateful for. They shared everything with us and each other. Having been as a child in a co-operative children's centre we had been encouraged to always be co-operative and to see equality and people's rights as central to how we should live, treating others with respect and acceptance for who and what they are and to see differences as a rich thing rather than a threat, helping each other along the way. It was part of everyday life in Mekelle and Wukro. This sort of stand was brought home to me even more when Linda Smith died recently, the comedienne. She was one of us from Sheffield and she wanted in her dying moments to help others, despite her own pain and suffering, and she and her partner gave money and asked that collections be made and sent to Wukro Children's Village. So you see death and personal loss as well is no barrier to helping others and to co-operation if you have a good and caring heart and see that all people are worthwhile to help and special.

Another story that is illustrative of the centre's international work in Ethiopia is that of Teberah, a young Ethiopian, adolescent woman who had been left behind when her father had fled Ethiopia and come to Britain as a political asylum seeker. Her father was in exile when he saw her, in the crowd, on television, in a programme about the famine. With the centre's help, and over a period of several months, her father was able to go through diplomatic and refugee channels to locate Teberah; the challenge was then to get her out of Ethiopia and bring her to England to live with her father. Centre workers supported the case by advocating with the relevant embassies and with the Home Office. A lengthy written submission was compiled, which made a case for reuniting Teberah with her family in Britain; her father had married and there were now two more children in the family. This took about 18 months and was eventually successful. Teberah spoke thus of her time in Ethiopia:

> I had experienced the worse of being a human being in the famine in Ethiopia, seeing babies, little children and adults starving before me and along with me, in conditions of total destruction and despair, but at that time I also experienced the absolute best in humanity through the hands of intervention and care and compassion through the actions of Maggie and the Children's Centre. Once you've been touched in this way by the worse of times it changes you for ever, you carry with you a fear, an apprehension that things can suddenly change for the worse but because I have also experienced acts of kindness and above-human efforts to save me and others, I always have hope and an awareness of the potential for goodness in all situations.

Teberah began to attend school in Sheffield and also attended the out-of-school provision at the centre. She progressed to becoming a volunteer at the centre and went on to pursue childcare qualifications with centre support, eventually becoming a paid worker at the centre. She undertook translation qualifications and worked as a translator. Eventually she came to own property in the city and continues to support the centre on a regular basis as part of its wide network of local and national contacts. In her reflection she had this to say about her own development and her feelings about the centre and its ongoing work:

> Even at the worse of times, I've seen it through other acts of the centre, that non-abandonment even when others, what's the English word, oh yeah, scarper, they stand firm beside you, that's why I wanted to give back to children and the centre, not just for my life but more importantly for the hope ... do you know what I mean? I translate for others and I feel every day that I need to succeed, to do my best in every way I can and to also be like a living testimony that helps others as well ... pass it on is the way, the unwritten motto I suppose.

## Working in Jordan

The initial contact for the Jordanian link came from a Jordanian woman who had a sector link with a member of the Pre-school Playgroups Association (PPA) in Sheffield (now the Pre-school Learning Alliance) and, through this, came to hear about the work of the centre and its potential to provide training courses across a range of areas. She made a visit to the centre.

Within Jordan, there had been an ongoing move in the kindergartens towards greater provision for play-based learning and a multicultural curriculum. To support this development, visits were subsequently made to the UK, by Jordanian practitioners, policy-makers and senior officials, to study curriculum provision, learning through play and intercultural engagement at the centre.

There were also associated prevailing issues in Jordan at this time relating to meeting the needs of a wide range of children, including disabled children and children who were experiencing traumas resulting from war and conflict and who were also refugees in the country. There were also recognised needs relating to children and adults with life-threatening illnesses. There was considerable interest in therapeutic play as a way forward for service development in Jordan. There was also a growing movement in Jordan that recognised the need to better understand structural inequalities in society and, within this, children's and women's rights as political dimensions associated with care and education for children, families and communities. The subsequent visit to the centre showed substantial common ground, and a way forward for working in partnership was initiated.

A training programme for Jordanian trainers was established by centre workers for delivery in Jordan. The intention was to use a cascade model for the development and improvement of services at local level. This programme looked at the established curriculum and the potential for introducing play-based learning. The programme addressed therapeutic play and also child and adult protection for women. This led to support for the development of women's aid services. Equality training was offered for workers and policy-makers. Through meetings and conferences held in Jordan, the centre workers connected and worked with senior politicians and policy-makers in the Ministry of Defence, the Ministry of Social Work, the Home Office and the Ministry of Youth, debating and gradually illustrating how provision for children and women was in the best interests of a nation. Presentations by centre workers were filmed for national television.

In developing programmes for disabled children, the centre workers began working with individual preschools (preschool is a term commonly used in Jordan). Staff from Jordan came over to Sheffield to work in the centre for extended periods and to gain qualifications, a model established during the Ethiopian work. Workers from Sheffield went over to model practice in the local settings. They too participated in conferences and seminars for academics and policy-makers, and also helped in producing publications on meeting disabled children's needs. These included the publication of practice guides, in Arabic, and the production of films as visual aids for training and development, and for awareness-raising with parents. Links were established with a women's organisation. This led to establishing and supporting early years provision in other areas of the country; once again the work was developing a momentum as it progressed, and expanding in its range and focus. It also progressed to supporting the development of economic co-operatives within the local communities. These were developing goods for sale to support economic self-sufficiency within those communities. The centre workers were also involved in supporting the development of literacy programmes, primarily for women. The extent of the importance of such programmes is captured in the following quote from Geeta Sharma in her article entitled 'UN Literacy Decade – hope or hype?':

The UN Literacy Decade Project has identified that there are one billion adults who cannot read and write. Out of this number, there are one hundred and fifteen million children out of school. Deputy UN Secretary General, Louise Frechette stated in February 2003 that: 'there is not a tool for development more effective than the education of girls and women'. UNESCO Director General Koichiro Matsuura, under whose direction the Decade project is coordinated, highlighted the importance of education and literacy by stating: 'through literacy, the downtrodden could find a voice, the poor could learn how to learn and the powerless could empower themselves. In that light, the drive for universal literacy was integrally linked to the human rights agenda. Literacy was not a universal panacea for all development problems but a tool for development; it was versatile and proven.

(http://learningchannel.oneworld.net/article/view/64045/1/12, accessed 11 March 2007)

As the work in Jordan progressed, the centre also worked with health provision in conjunction with physiotherapists, occupational therapists and doctors. This work was undertaken on an individual casework basis in relation to the assessment of and the meeting of children's impairment requirements. This approach was supported by an awareness-raising programme with professionals and with local communities in Jordan. Disabled children in Jordan at this time, as in many other parts of the world, were being engaged with through a medical model of disability, which served to exclude and disempower them from the mainstream and from experiencing ordinary lives. This programme promoted a social model of anti-discrimination and inclusion, in which it was recognised that children and adults with impairments are disabled by society; this is manifest through policy, attitudes, restricted access, inappropriate environments and other forms of dis-ableism. The centre's work had always recognised that many individuals have or subsequently acquire impairments whose requirements can easily be met – for example, a short-sighted person needing glasses. In contrast to this, a view still prevails that disabled children need only special toys when a social model would argue that many toys can be adapted to suit all children, regardless of their impairment requirements or age or stage of development. These ideas relating to inclusion and public participation and decision-making were shared through the developing programmes in Jordan. Disabled staff from the centre worked in Jordan as positive role models. Gradually, centre workers began to see an increase in the numbers of disabled children attending the local services.

As time went on, cross-cultural links were formed between children in Sheffield and children in Jordan. This was integrated in Sheffield into the emerging work at the Shack (discussed in Chapter 4). The children and young people were sharing ideas on childhood culture and their daily lives in each country. They made films about art and craft activities, and undertook performances that reflected local, popular culture, from rap to Arabic dancing. Children in each country made films about children's rights and, in Jordan and Sheffield, these films were used to engage with local government. The children and young people from Sheffield spoke at the House of Commons and the Museum of Me in London to lobby on children's rights. Some of the children and young people in Jordan performed at a national conference centre for members of the royal family and the Jordanian Government.

Leading on from this, the children and young people in Jordan were given a piece of land in Amman to develop their own 'Shack' and this was then linked to other established projects that had evolved in Jordan through the links with the centre. The small beginnings had gradually, and over time, transformed into an international liaison between children and young people, which allowed them to share arts and culture and to look at commonalities and differences from a range of Arab and international backgrounds. The Arab world covers an area twice the size of Europe, stretching across continents, and is hugely diverse and multicultural. These initiatives fed into the development of cultural identity for children and young people in both these locations as those in Jordan saw how Arabic and other cultures were expressed in England, and as the children and young people in England began to see the multiple faces of Arabic culture as expressed in Jordan.

While working in Jordan the centre was approached by members of the Palestinian community living there. They requested assistance with issues they were facing, with children and families having lived for long periods in temporary camps. The centre was asked if it could work to support disabled children in two particular refugee camps. Sheffield hospitals supported this work through aid and resources sent across for children with cerebral palsy and other impairment requirements. The centre also worked with senior figures to introduce conductive education for disabled children. The centre set up a cross-cultural health link with a Sheffield hospice to facilitate palliative care methods in Jordan for children and adults. Healthcare staff from Jordan came to Sheffield to work at the local hospice and also at the Sheffield Children's Centre, to access training and experience to cascade back into the camps and throughout Jordan. The Jordanian Prime Minister's wife also visited Sheffield and the centre, and was very active in the disabled children's movement in Jordan.

## Working in Pakistan

From its earliest days the Sheffield Children's Centre has been developing links with Pakistan arising from service users' and workers' family, community and professional links in the country. This work extended in the mid-1990s when Noor (a centre worker born and with family connections in the area) and Jenny undertook a reconnaissance visit to Azad Kashmir. It became apparent to them very quickly that there were urgent medical and nutritional needs for those living in the camps. In one refugee camp, groups of refugees felt that one of their most urgent needs was clean water. Centre workers and supporters endeavoured to support them in moving forward with this aspiration; this included bringing in an engineer to help them access clean water. Money was raised via voluntary contributions in the UK and much of this is sustained through sponsorship and fundraising activities by centre workers, service users (including children) and supporters.

In this camp also, Noor and Jenny undertook an extended consultation with all community members on their resource needs and aspirations for community and environment development. The primary aspiration was for a mosque to be established. The mosque is not only a place of worship but also a symbol of the community heartland. The centre and its workers recognised that a positive response to this request on their part had the potential to be a 'political minefield'. They were aware from their conversations with other aid workers in the region that there were different points of view on how aid work should go forward.

However, their principles of practice include listening to the community and responding to its members' perceived needs in supporting the spiritual growth and well-being of a community in distress and need. In seeking to uphold this principle they responded positively and raised funds to help in building the mosque. They saw how the focus began to create and cement a stronger sense of community and of local identity among the local people, and how it created a shared commitment to collective forward-looking and renewal. The mosque was used for spiritual, educational and community purposes. The fundraising also provided beads, prayer mats, copies of the Koran, medical aid, sewing machines, buffaloes (which provide more milk than cows and also provide butter and ghee) and many other resources that the community requested. Workers took the funds across for the work and made videos as testament to the work and its impact. They supported camp members in applying for and gaining identity cards as this would help them gain jobs and increase the family income. As time passed, they began supporting other local communities in building mosques also, having been approached by these communities because of word of mouth. They continue today to support the camps and local communities, and to maintain the established networks and links.

In 2005, there was a huge earthquake across the Pakistan/Kashmir border, close to the area where Noor had family links and where the centre had already been working. Noor flew across to the area and was appalled by the conditions in which local people were living. Children were attempting to survive without their parents, there was no food or shelter, and children and adults were dying in the ruins as no help was forth-coming for them. Noor heard many stories from local people that prompted her to want to help. She rang the workers at the centre, who began to fundraise in the local community in Sheffield. Noor made links with an older boy who was attempting to help other children, and tried to focus her efforts on assisting with relief for the children. The boy, now a young man, is currently working at the centre. The fundraising had mixed success; some local firms and shops in Sheffield subscribed but others said it was not their policy to do so. Parents and workers at the centre raised funds and members of the local community contributed. One worker said she and her family went home to turn out pockets and bags, and were surprised at the amount of loose change they found. They went to the local radio station to make an appeal to raise funds. In four days they raised enough money for tents and food, and to bring in a team from Pakistan to begin recovering bodies. Noor flew back to England, then returned to the area with the funds and aid, and began organising support. Trucks were hired to distribute food, baby milk, water and children's clothes. A shipment of tents was flown out – 'the basics to survive' as Maggie commented in a magazine feature (*Nursery World*, 2005). They raised enough money to bring in a doctor. From this personal link, and these small and hurriedly convened beginnings, a local project was emerging that is still working in the area today. The relief camp became a place in which schools emerged, and in which local doctors and local people began to work and support community members, based on the same model of development that had underpinned their other work in the area. Centre workers linked with other local and regional disaster relief initiatives in Britain to support areas such as Bagh (which was severely hit). Maggie supported the fundraising efforts of other groups active in the disaster area through formulating fundraising strategies, funding bids and assisting with funding events.

It is this philosophy, an integral part of the centre's *heartland*, that creates the *catalyst for change* at a local level, both nationally, and, as we have seen in this chapter, internationally also. It operates in sharp contrast to bureaucratic directives and requirement to meet targets.

In pursuing these links, centre workers had also established local and national links with a number of mosques in Sheffield, and had taken advice in relation to the visits to Pakistan and the related work with children and families there. This work remained relatively small scale until the centre received a written request for support from children's services at national level in Pakistan. The centre's ongoing work had come to their attention through word of mouth and they wished to pursue a more formal partnership that would expand the work of the centre in Pakistan.

Word of mouth also worked in the opposite direction. For example, when a senior official from Luton Borough Council visited Pakistan, he heard about the work of the centre. Centre workers were subsequently invited to con-tribute to the children and families' agenda in Luton, with an emphasis on early years, childcare and play service development, and anti-racist and multicultural service development for children and families. The centre was presented with a civic award for its work in Luton by the then Lord Mayor of Luton, Councillor Waheed Akbar who wished to 'acknowledge the wonderful contribution the centre has made to the lives of children, families and communities in Luton and other cities and towns throughout Britain and internationally'.

## Working with Zimbabwe

The Batanai Project in Zimbabwe was started by the late and legendary Auxillia Chimusoro in 1992, in Rujeko township in Masvingo town. It was started by people with HIV/AIDS in order to provide mutual support within the local community. Batanai seeks to promote the human rights of people living with HIV, and to combat prejudice and discrimination. Its website identifies that, currently, more than 30 per cent of the adult population is HIV positive. More than 35 per cent of pregnant women are HIV positive. Approximately 12 per cent of children are HIV positive, mostly due to maternal infections with some due to sexual abuse of children by HIV-positive men and women. Currently, around 2500 people die every week of AIDS-related illnesses. The number of orphans will soon reach one million.

Auxillia came to visit the centre during 1992 when she herself had AIDS; she had heard about the work of the centre from centre workers with whom she was speaking casually at a conference on HIV in Sheffield. The centre then linked with the Batanai branch of the project in Sheffield to support the project's aims and objectives, and to undertake practical work with them in relation to their work in Zimbabwe and their worldwide awareness-raising of HIV/AIDS. They fundraised on their behalf and acted as a conduit for the sale of goods – tablecloths, lace and cardigans – made by local groups with HIV/AIDS in Zimbabwe.

One of the fathers at the centre, of African-Caribbean heritage, formed especial links with the project. He was a specialist worker in HIV/AIDS and was particularly keen to support the centre in getting actively involved in this project. He saw it as having dual benefit for people in Sheffield and in Zimbabwe, and was able to provide a focal point for the centre's involvement in the project and to help create some momentum and cohesion in the emerging activities, links and initiatives.

Batanai Zimbabwe, with the support of Batanai Sheffield, began to undertake awareness-raising activities in Europe. One of these was the establishing of a touring theatre company that performed set pieces around HIV/AIDS for adults and children in local communities. This group also made a presentation to the World Health Organization in Geneva.

Following Auxillia's death, her son, Fraie, a community health promotion worker who was part of the Batanai Zimbabwe Sheffield project, spent some time working voluntarily at Sheffield Children's Centre, linking with health projects, raising awareness of sexual health in the community and combating discrimination towards people with HIV/AIDS. He took over the role and work of his mother, linking with the wider world and including in this work the Sheffield Children's Centre.

The centre, through its film-making work, produced a film about children with HIV/AIDS in Zimbabwe and Britain. The film was shown in Belgium and other European countries as part of a children's mini-documentary film festival. It was also shown in Africa by Batanai Zimbabwe and through the other African links established by the centre. Once the film-making had been completed, the children and young people at Sheffield Children's Centre, who had fundraised to purchase this equipment, decided to donate it to children and young people-linked projects in Zimbabwe for their use in promoting their issues and concerns, both HIV/AIDS related and beyond.

Before moving on from these examples of international local projects with which the centre has been associated, it is also worth briefly mentioning work in Somalia with children, young people and women's groups, supporting the establishment of salt-making co-operatives to a stand-alone status. This work was ongoing over a three-year period.

## Survivors of institutional child abuse

South Yorkshire has a substantial number of survivors of institutional child abuse living in the area. The institutions concerned consisted of schools, reformatories, hospitals and orphanages within the Irish Republic, mainly run by religious orders from the turn of the century until the 1970s. Through working with children and families throughout the region, from the Irish and Irish Traveller community, the centre workers, some of whom are also from the Irish and Irish Traveller community, became aware of the survivors' needs and the experiences they had suffered as children. Working with some of the survivors the centre began to establish support networks from the mid-1980s onwards.

Tony O'Farrell is a survivor of the Artane Industrial School in Dublin, where it is now recognised that substantial abuse of boys took place. He has documented these experiences in his book, *The Silent Cry*, for which he is seeking a publisher. Tony began doing unpaid work with the centre, supporting families and members of the wider community on issues of employment and rights. He was also a founding member of Irish SOCA (Survivors of Child Abuse). He began working with Chrissy Meleady in lobbying the Irish Government on behalf of survivors to formulate a Commission for Inquiry on Child Abuse, and to make reparation and redress past injustices while reflecting on future child protection matters in Ireland. The Commission for Inquiry on Child Abuse was finally established in 1999 by the Irish Government. With the support of CM, Tony O'Farrell made a formal submission to the Commission on behalf of Irish SOCA in respect of giving consideration to definitions being applied to issues of assault and injuries sustained by the children in the care of religious orders. The rationale for this was that older British legislation from 1861 was being applied in terms of defining abuse as 'common assault', which is a legal but lesser term applying to non-physical injury with no bruising. It could include a shove but could not be applied to any sexual contact/invasion. Survivors sustained assault and abuse far in excess of the definition in use of 'common assault'. This was argued in the submission by Tony to the Commission of Inquiry, along with other points of contention. A summary plea emphasised the plight of the children and young people subjected to the abuse in the following concluding section:

> As children, we were solely pre-occupied with a fight for survival and self-protection in conditions of danger, grinding poverty and ill-health. We were neglected, exploited, abused, treated with cruelty by adults, many from religious orders who had taken vows of poverty, chastity and obedience with an added vow to preserve the vocation and teach gratuitously. We call upon all concerned to evade obstacles to affirmative investigation and to effect changes to allow our childhood and now adult voices to be heard without restraint and with free expression and with appropriate support. We feel that the Commission is evading this through its process of extending privilege and immunity of evidence requested by religious orders.

The submission concluded by asking the Commission to designate an increase in fees for the survivors for their legal costs in making representation to the Commission, which would be comparable to that given by the Commission to the parties being accused of child abuse.

In conclusion, the submission from Irish SOCA states: 'we ask the Commission to view our position with fairness and equality and to remember the children we once were, whose childhood was stolen from us'.

Tentative recognition was given to the document, but its substantive pleas, it was understood, would upset the balance already achieved by the Commission. The Commission is continuing to operate in relation to hearing cases of child abuse in institutional settings. All of the above continue to work on these matters. Tony continues to support intergenerational work at the centre, and supports in relation to issues of adult abuse across the city as an expert elder.

One case is illustrative of the work that was undertaken through the partnerships and links in this area. Irish SOCA became aware of the early release from prison of a religious brother jailed for child abuse. He had served 18 months of a 36-year sentence for sexually assaulting children over a 20-year period. The circuit judge who authorised the brother's release issued a banning order requiring the man to leave Ireland and not return. He was to be deported to England. Contact was made with the Home Secretary in connection with this to ask why this was deemed appropriate. The Home Secretary referred the matter to the international section of Scotland Yard. As a consequence, the offender was restricted from entering the UK but it was believed he was then considering entering Belgium as a place of residence. Further challenge was extended and we understand he was refused entry to Belgium. The following February, in Ireland, this man, now aged 75, was charged with a further 77 offences against children and was given an additional five-year custodial sentence, serving only one year.

Within Sheffield, the centre has worked with the Catholic cathedral clergy, who have been very responsive to this agenda. Together, they have organised reflective events for survivors, non-abusing clergy and lay members of the Catholic faith to nurture past, present and future healing. Other aspects of this joint working have included racial justice events and Holocaust memorial activities. The joint working has also included *porraimos* commemorations. (*Porraimos* means 'the devouring', and refers to the genocide of Roma Gypsies during the Nazi regime.) In addition, the centre, the Catholic cathedral and Sheffield Racial Equality Council have worked together to roll out and embed Heartstone's Descendants of All Worlds programme. Heartstone is an international organisation working towards eliminating racism and xenophobia using visual media and performing arts to convey its message through stories.

Sheffield Children's Centre has also supported the work of CAFOD, the Catholic Agency for Overseas Development. CAFOD works to further social justice in over 60 countries, regardless of race or religion, and centre workers and service users of all races and denominations have supported this work through fundraising.

## Chapter summary

This chapter has presented and discussed examples of international initiatives that have developed in the centre's work. In many cases, these links have emerged in the first instance though 'word of mouth', a facet of service development we have seen in previous chapters as also influencing the emergence and development of the centre's local work. The centre workers do not see themselves as geographically bounded and as opportunities to continue service provision present themselves, they challenge themselves to respond and to identify cultural appropriateness in their work in these new contexts. They are guided in this through application of fundamental principles based around 'hearing the voice of the community' to guide the design and delivery of the emerging services. They may find themselves in unfamiliar territory in terms of service development, responding to local communities that are very differently constituted and living in very different social, economic and political climates than those they are more familiar with in England. But, as we have seen, they do not back away from unfamiliarity. Not all workers are involved in the international initiatives but become so as they wish and as they feel comfortable, and we have seen that participation extends to young service users also.

The flat management structure and collaborative principles undoubtedly aid their capacity for rapid response and forward movement in these contexts, along with the gradually accumulated knowledge and understanding of the more long-standing workers in initiating the range of activities and in leading other workers forward in their implementation. They learn on the job and acknowledge that, where once they might have acted from commitment but relative naivety, the commitment leads them to a more informed level of participation and support for other communities; their principles become newly informed and expanded. Freed from the boundaries of a managerial hierarchy, the centre workers become strong networkers with a resource of cumulative knowledge on how to initiate and generate new types of service provision in new contexts; over time, they have accumulated a body of knowledge upon which they are prepared to act, and this becomes an integral part of their social and cultural capital, which allows them to open up and service this reciprocal highway. They build knowledge and expertise as they go and, in linking into and developing services in international contexts, they feed back into the knowledge and understanding of the adults and the children and young people associated with the centre.

Their networks and shared principles for practice and action draw in a wide range of individuals who participate in the international initiatives in different ways and for different lengths of time. This accumulated participation adds momentum to the work and helps sustain impact and development over time as local capacity grows and as local people in the international settings become more expert at developing and maintaining the services themselves. In this way, centre workers aim to build and expand capacity rather than to create dependency, and seek wherever possible to work with local and national governments to establish and maintain a supportive infrastructure; it is the local model in action internationally and illustrates the transferability of principles and practice in related contexts.

A key unifying construct for the centre's work is perhaps that of *empowerment*, manifest locally and internationally through the following principles of practice:

- the intention to offer practical advice for problem-solving
- the intention to give informed support at key times
- the determination to give the disenfranchised a voice and the means to be heard
- the intention to take a non-judgemental approach to the circumstances of individuals, of families and of communities
- a recognition of the need for equity and parity in management and leadership structures
- an acknowledgement that in confronting personal difficulties every individual acquires skills to share with others
- a fundamental recognition of all aspects of diversity being integral to community life
- a realisation and understanding of the strengths brought from multicultural, multi-ethnic and gender-balanced teams
- a belief that people, including the disenfranchised, can take control of their lives and enrich the common good
- a belief that social justice and anti-discrimination are well worth constructing in the local and broader ethos
- a belief that individuals and communities do know what they need, and that their voices should be heard and acted upon.

These principles of practice, when transferred to work in international contexts, just as with the centre's earlier work in Sheffield, create the potential for the growth of project identities elsewhere. Some of this work – for example, the work in Ethiopia – also grew from dimensions of resistance identity in that local Ethiopian people sought to be proactive in the face of bureaucratic impassiveness to the plight of children and families. Other work comes initiated by senior personnel within the mainstream, but nevertheless must still confront established boundaries of practice through new kinds of action and interaction, as in the centre's work in Jordan and Pakistan. As can be seen from the work on institutional child abuse, the centre workers are prepared to confront government representatives if they believe actions to be inappropriate or dangerous.

These are firm stances to take and the workers at the centre have been taking them over an extended period, learning as they go and so creating an internal energy and a dynamic that sustains their commitment to the work, even through periods of confrontation and difficulty. The next and final chapter brings the centre's work back home, and looks to the past and the future in the conclusion to this story of Sheffield Children's Centre.

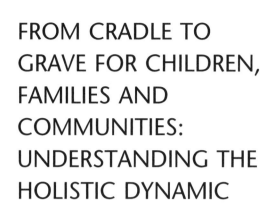

# FROM CRADLE TO GRAVE FOR CHILDREN, FAMILIES AND COMMUNITIES: UNDERSTANDING THE HOLISTIC DYNAMIC

This chapter opens by telling a little more of the story, to date, of the centre's aspirations and activities for growth and development, building on its Early Excellence Centre status awarded in 1999. The chapter and the book then conclude with a conceptualisation of the centre's work by interconnecting the key ideas and themes that have provided the conceptual framework for describing the centre's evolution. Our broader aim here is to examine the potential of the centre for informing the wider, national, and potentially international, development of services for children and families, bearing in mind the phrase so aptly quoted by Peter Moss in the Foreword: 'a "local cultural project of childhood" ... a recognition of public responsibility to local children as valued citizens of their community, and a commitment, sustained over time, to giving culturally appropriate meaning to that responsibility'.

It seems important to set these two aspects – the aspiration for development and the potential for wider influence – alongside one another in this final chapter. The first part illuminates the determination of the centre to flourish and its attempts to secure growth, while the second illustrates how the centre and its work might substantially expand social theory in relation to community-based services for children and families.

In describing some of the centre's attempts to grow and develop (we do not have space for all of them here) we draw substantially from documents in the public domain. We use these texts to illustrate the more recent dilemmas and difficulties faced by the centre as government policy has evolved and been interpreted and applied by the local authority. In terms of centre development, this chapter focuses most substantially on its attempts to purchase adjoining land in order to house the expanding services in a much needed new centre and, as a consequence, to remain connected to government policy developments, in particular the emerging programme of Children's Centres, within which it seemed to Sheffield Children's Centre, it had a substantial contribution to make.

Inevitably there has been some selectivity in the choice of documents that have been drawn upon here, driven most substantially by a need to be concise and coherent in telling this part of the story. We have endeavoured to remain balanced, conscious that this book is not the time or place to lay blame in relation to the difficulties that the centre has experienced in seeking to develop and expand its services. As the story of the centre unfolds, some of its ongoing difficulties are documented. In particular, it becomes apparent that its dialogues with local authority representatives on the purchase of the necessary land and in relation to its potential inclusion in the rapidly developing world of the newly emerging national Children's Centres have been especially difficult. We tell this part of the story not in a spirit of accusation, in any respect, but to be illustrative of the challenges that need to be overcome by a community-based organisation that operates within co-operative principles and that seeks to remain vibrant and viable in a changing world.

## Part 1: more recent developments at Sheffield Children's Centre

When the centre was awarded Early Excellence Centre status in 1999, the accompanying grant from the government pool had been £83,000, to be used mainly for staff costs. This money came directly to the centre. For the year 2002/03 the centre had requested an increased EEC grant for continued staffing and for other aspects of service development. This increased grant was eventually awarded in that year and in the following two years, demonstrating quite clearly the government's view that this was a worthwhile and important community service. However, the funding allocations were not without delays and difficulties along the way. A letter from Margaret Hodge to David Blunkett (as a Sheffield MP) and relating to the centre, dated September 2004, is worth considering. In general terms, it highlights the uncertainties associated with government funding for community providers. The letter also gives a clear indication of emerging government expectations relating to the forward movement of EECs as Children's Centres came on stream. It was this forward movement within which the centre aspired to participate as a recognised Children's Centre. The letter stated:

> There were difficulties with the administration of the scheme (EEC) in 2003 following internal re-structuring and the departure of all the existing team (referring here to within government office). This led to unacceptably long delays for some centres in the approval of their grant. Sheffield Children's Centre was one of these. Payments were however made 'on account' for the first 2 quarters but then had to be suspended

once they exceeded the level of the indicative allocation for the centre. It was not clear that the higher amount could be made because of a number of pressures on the budget that were unresolved. I am pleased to say that it has been possible to pay the final balance to the centre.

Turning now to the plan for 04/05 that the centre submitted on 7 May 2004, I should explain that there were concerns about some of the planned activities and my officials met with Chrissy Meleady [CM] to discuss these in July. We are strongly encouraging existing programmes, such as the EECs, to position themselves as best they can now, using their current funding, to provide building blocks to deliver children's centre services in the future. This means concentrating on providing services that deliver the children's centre core offer.

I am aware that the Sheffield Children's Centre has not been included in the local authority's plans for their first 'wave' of children's centres. I know that Chrissy Meleady is in discussion with the local authority herself about this and the Sure Start Unit's regional team will do all they can to facilitate these discussions. We do want to build on good existing provision and expertise to develop children's centre services and the work the Sheffield Children's Centre has done delivering early education and care to the families in Sheffield has been recognised as high quality.

There are three points to be made in relation to the centre's development in this key period of government expansion of services. First, the government grant was for staffing and new workers had been appointed to the centre, however the subsequent period of uncertainty about continuity of funding had meant that there were times when the centre had had to carry costs for new workers until further funding was agreed and forthcoming from the government office. Such financial uncertainties have considerable implications for sustainability for independent service providers who do not have the bolster of additional funding streams as local authorities do. The loss of entire administrative teams in government departments clearly puts independent providers at huge risk also as continuities in funding are threatened. Second, children and family providers were being steered towards the 'core offer' for Children's Centres in order to establish their right to be designated. In August 2003, the Sure Start guidance had identified six aspects to the core offer:

1. early education integrated with daycare
2. family support and parental outreach
3. child and family health services
4. links with schools and the Children's Information Services
5. links with Jobcentre Plus
6. other links and services including with further and higher education and trainers, training for parents, specialist services for children with disabilities, benefits advice, childcare and other services for older children.

While Sheffield Children's Centre may not have been offering all these services in the exact way envisaged at that time by government, we believe the previous chapters testify to it having already established many of the services in response to community need, in the preceding years; indeed this expanded service provision was integral to its designation as an EEC. Despite this, and despite the ministerial 'steer' towards core offer activity, as stated in the letter, the centre was finding it difficult to feature to any considerable extent in local authority plans for the first wave of Children's Centre roll-out.

The third point relating to the letter concerns the minister's acknowledgement of the 'essential part' to be played by the Sure Start regional team in facilitating links between the centre and the local authority. PB, as the EEC evaluator, and CM, as the then Chair of the Management Committee, had spoken with the Sure Start regional team leader in Leeds in November 2002. The team leader had confirmed at this meeting that no capital funding relating to government initiatives would be forthcoming to the centre. She had based this statement on information that she had received from senior officers in the local authority and arising from a previous strategy meeting in the city. She had remarked that funding would be provided by the local authority for ongoing developments to a nursery school about half a mile from the centre – one that the authority subsequently closed several months later. Interestingly, this was also the nursery school from which local parents had removed their children during the early days of the St Mary's Community Programme because of the many perceived aspects of cultural inappropriateness that parents had felt were evident in the nursery school.

Linked to this third point, and in response to emerging government policy, the local authority subsequently decided in 2003 to adopt a 'hub and satellite' approach to the first-wave development of Children's Centres. The hub would be a single location/centre providing some services and central administration. The satellites would work in partnership to complement the hub and be located in the near vicinity. Sheffield would receive £4,005,046 capital funding and £1,332,138 for revenue development, with an aim to develop 13 Children's Centres in the 20 per cent, designated, most deprived wards across the city. A Sharrow Sure Start/Local Authority Board Paper entitled 'Capital options paper' was formulated, and referenced the centre alongside other potential first-wave providers. It identified options and made proposals for Children's Centre designation. In relation to the Sheffield Children's Centre it identified as strengths its early excellence status, its large number of active projects and its accessibility – considerable strengths one might think. However, this document also identified that the centre 'lacked any engagement over the past eight months', 'plans for a new building [were] uncertain' and there was 'limited space in the existing building' – issues that, as the following discussion will illustrate, the centre had been trying to address with the local authority for some time. The recommendation in this 'Capital options paper' relating to the centre was that 'this matter is left pending', ultimately leaving the centre in a continuing state of uncertainty as to any potential inclusion in local authority developments.

In 2003, an existing maintained nursery school, some three miles (as the crow flies) from Sheffield Children's Centre was identified as the proposed location of the hub for the area being served by Sheffield Children's Centre, the Sharrow area. This was despite the fact that, in the above-mentioned document (the 'Capital options paper'), this particular nursery school's weaknesses were identified as having an 'intrangient [sic] history', as having 'limited impact on the local community' and that there was 'a risk that the traditional nursery will find change difficult'. The ultimate recommendation in this document was that this nursery school be progressed as the satellite, with the caveat that 'strategies are put in place to ensure use by the local community'. This nursery school became the first-phase Children's Centre to incorporate the area being served by Sheffield Children's Centre, with the majority of other city areas to be served by this 'new' Children's Centre to include some of the most affluent parts of the city. By 2006, it had been decided by the local authority that the local primary school in Sharrow would combine with the local Sure Start Programme then recently established in the Sharrow area to provide the designated Children's Centre in the Sharrow area within second-phase roll-out. Sheffield Children's Centre was not included in these strategic developments.

Two years previously, in 2004, the centre had received a letter from a senior officer of the authority stating: 'The Children's Centre strategy for Sheffield, as agreed at Cabinet, proposed capital spend to be directed mainly to non Sure Start areas and in the Sharrow ward, no Children's Centre capital is required.' It is not known whether capital was subsequently spent on the new Sharrow development but it did seem to the management committee and to centre workers that a trail of mixed messages was all that was forthcoming as deliberations continued and as local decision-making was implemented by the City Council.

Let us go back in time at this point and detail the centre's activities in seeking to purchase land and further develop its service provision in this changing climate of national and local policy development.

In 1998, the Sheffield Children's Centre had been looking to redevelopment opportunities. Its aim was to provide purpose-built accommodation for the now expanded community services developed over the years since its move to the present location. As stated previously, it had also been acknowledged during the EEC period that the premises in which the centre was located were deemed no longer suitable for purpose: the buildings would soon not be fit for purpose. The centre's management committee had decided to approach the local authority for the purpose of acquiring some land adjoining the centre, permanently unused, and for the associated development of a new centre, for which detailed architectural plans were drawn up and paid for from the centre's budget (not EEC funding). With the capital allocation of £250,000 from the centre's EEC designation, centre staff also needed to seek additional funding to supplement the DfES grant. It was made clear by the DfES that the capital spend would not be transferred until the land acquisition was complete, and sufficient complementary funding was in place to begin the new development.

In 1998, representatives of the management committee met with the Council Leader and the Works Department to discuss the land purchase for the first time. In the lead-up to the designation of EEC status, DfES representatives had made it clear that new premises would be required at some point in the near future. The management committee was advised to approach senior officers within the Local Education Authority to pursue its request. This was to be the first of many related meetings. Because of the difficulties the centre subsequently faced in their negotiations with the City Council in relation to the land purchase, the DfES subsequently took the unprecedented step of carrying over this capital grant, beyond the life of EECs, after first also carrying it over, twice, on an annual basis. Once again, this seems to indicate government support for maintaining and developing this independent service.

The following chronology documents and summarises the activities of the management committee and associates over an extended period in trying to progress the purchase of the land adjoining the Sheffield Children's Centre for the development of a new build.

## Chronology of events

### February 1999

A request is made for a second meeting with council representatives in relation to the land, and an agreement is made by them to send a senior officer from educational services to the centre. No one came. In July, the centre requested Property Services to value the land. An officer came to look but nothing was subsequently presented in writing or verbally. In August, a further meeting took place with the newly elected Council Leader and Chair of the Education Committee. They said senior officers from education would visit. None did. The centre's management committee wanted to bid for funding from other streams coming available at that time to complement the £250,000 received through the EEC capital funding grant. They could not do so until they knew that they would have access to the adjoining land. In September a business plan for site development (subject to land access) was sent to Young Children's Services, including detailed plans for the proposed development. The preparation costs were carried by the centre. The proposal was for a two-floor centre with designated training/meeting rooms and local community services. No response was received. Nevertheless, centre representatives began initial discussions with potential funders for the new initiative in the hope that the land issue would be resolved.

### October 2000

CM and PB made a presentation to the local authority Early Years Development and Childcare Partnership on the centre's work as an EEC and its capacity to meet government targets within the local community in relation to early years and family support service developments. In addition, the Black Community Forum and Sheffield Racial Equality Council advocated on behalf of the centre with the local authority, in relation to the land acquisition and to partnership development between the centre and the city. The centre was being urged to progress the land acquisition by DfES. In November 2000, there was another meeting with the Leader of the Council to which the site architect also made a presentation (PB was also present). A comprehensive business plan and detailed architectural study were left and it was agreed that these documents would be transferred to the relevant council departments.

Time elapsed and there was no response from the City Council or its representatives; another letter was written. A promised link person to connect the centre and the city never materialised; there was still no information about the land. In 2001, the local authority was notified by the centre that there was now a real risk of the allocated capital funding designated through EEC being lost as the DfES indicated that it could be reclaimed. This represented a potential loss of services within this disadvantaged ward.

## June 2002

After repeated requests, and not until June 2002, another meeting with another new Council Leader and with the Director of Services for Education was arranged. It was attended instead by the Cabinet Lead for Education and an Assistant Director of Educational Services, by workers from the centre and by PB. An email from a DfES representative detailing the potential loss of the capital funding of £250,000 was tabled and it was reiterated that other potential funders would not commit to the development project unless the land matter was clear. These difficulties were recognised at this meeting and it was agreed they would be addressed immediately by the authority. It was also pointed out at the meeting that the centre had been told it could not apply for Objective 1 funding as it lay outside the designated boundary for authorised bidding to this fund by 300 yards. Objective 1 funding was designated for city centre regeneration and the centre's management committee had identified this as a key source of additional income for the development plans. It was also acknowledged that Sheffield Children's Centre was the only childcare, early education and family support provider to serve the city centre. It was suggested by officers at this meeting that a further meeting be convened with the Council Leader and the Chief Executive as they had jurisdiction over boundaries relating to Objective 1 funding.

## October 2002

The centre was invited to and representatives attended an Area Planning Meeting. This is a key forum for public consultation in local decision-making. A presentation was made by centre staff relating to a Neighbourhood Nurseries Initiative (NNI) bid by the centre as an additional strategy in securing funding for service development. NNIs were a further government initiative started in 2001 to provide accessible and affordable daycare in the poorest areas. Centre workers were also still hoping at this point to negotiate some level of participation in the new Sure Start Local Programme that had by now been located in the Sharrow ward and was situated close to the centre. It was agreed verbally by panel members that the NNI bid should be supported, but this agreement did not appear in the minutes of the meeting. There would not be another Area Planning Meeting until February 2003. PB and CM requested an opportunity to present to the local Sure Start Board on the EEC evaluation findings and possible links, and this was undertaken in December 2002 despite the fact that in the previous month, as stated above, the Sure

Start regional team leader had already confirmed to CM and PB that there were no plans to include the centre in this ongoing work.

## November 2002

The centre received two letters relating to the land purchase in this month. The letters appeared to have contradictory messages. One was from the Council Leader. It referred back to the difficulties in being considered for Objective 1 funding, for which the centre had been trying to arrange a further meeting having been told at a previous meeting (at which PB was also present) that the Council Leader and Chief Executive had jurisdiction over boundaries and needed to be consulted. This first letter, from the Council Leader, seemed to be contradicting a view that this was where the jurisdiction for grant allocation lay. It stated:

> You ask me whether the council would support your Objective 1 application. Well, we do not take a view one way or the other – you need to make your application and it will be assessed against your business plan. If the Objective 1 secretariat make an in principle award, then let us know, at least you will be well on your way to securing what is required.
> Of course I cannot make any undertaking formally on behalf of the Council, but if you achieved your capital funding I would be arguing for a land transfer at nil consideration (it would be brilliant of course if you could get a capital receipt from your external funders but perhaps a tad optimistic).

There is an evident Catch 22 here: get the funding assured and you can have the land, while you can't have funding without the assurance of land transfer! In the previous September, the centre had received a request for further information in relation to its business plan and bid for capital and revenue support under the NNI; this included reference to the importance of securing the land purchase and producing proof of matched funding; progress, it seemed, could not be made on the issue of the land.

Also in November 2002, the centre received the second letter relating to the land acquisition. It was a five-page document from the Head of Access and Inclusion at the City Council. It had a rather contradictory tone to the letter detailed above from the Council Leader. This second letter gave a figure for the purchase of land of £250,000 as 'a way forward' – coincidentally, the exact amount the DfES was making available for the capital project and to which the council's attention had been drawn in a tabled email a few months earlier. The letter requested that the centre demonstrate that funding was in place for the proposed development work, something that was continuing to prove impossible without a confirmation that the land would be transferred. The letter was critical of the centre for not previously disclosing the cost of the site; despite repeated requests for this information, this was the first time any costs had been associated with the site by the City Council.

*What happened next?*

The chronology stopped at this point. It was circulated to local MPs, City Council members and others as an attempt to highlight the continued difficulties being experienced by the centre in making progress in relation to the land acquisition. A reply was received from the Right Honourable David Blunkett MP, then Home Secretary, dated December 2002 and agreeing to look into the matter; a further exchange of letters ensued.

The Chief Executive of the City Council subsequently wrote to David Blunkett defending aspects of their actions and, from their perspective, correcting perceived inaccuracies in the chronology. He stated that stipulated and referenced requests for meetings were not evident in their files but also stated that the head of service in post at that time was no longer in post. It was stated that the files held no record of a business plan submitted in September 1999, although there was a reference later in the letter to a received business plan, although it was not clear in the letter if these were references to the same business plan. The letter also stated that there was no record of DfES representatives requesting land matters be progressed. Another point stated that there was no submission to the NNI initiative in 2002, although later in the letter reference is made to a 'capital bid of £190K to NNI' as a small proportion of a 'proposed £5 million development'. The letter states that two meetings arranged with the centre had been cancelled by the centre during the period.

Having had little success in the first-wave roll-out of Children's Centres, the workers and management committee nevertheless persisted in aiming for participation in the second-wave roll-out. They made repeated requests for meetings and discussion, and for participation in the wider roll-out taking place during July 2004. On 22 July, two local authority officers visited the centre by invitation to be received by CM and in the presence of a legal case worker from Sheffield Racial Equality Council (SREC). The draft note produced and circulated by email from one local authority officer after this visit stated that '[Lead officer] accepted that there might be some credence in what previously happened to SCC but unfortunately that was in the past', referring here to the difficulties in securing the land and in relation to greater participation in local authority service development. On 2 August 2004, full local authority notes of the visit were issued, which omitted the senior officer's comments about the past events. The onus was placed on CM and on the management committee to continue seeking information about possible future involvement in the roll-out of Children's Centres. The notes stated that in the forthcoming autumn term, another stakeholder meeting for key providers in Sharrow would be held and CM would be invited to become involved with the Children's Centre Strategy; this never transpired.

In relation to the outstanding sum of £250,000 and its carry-over, an email from a DfES representative, dated 25 April 2005, confirmed the continued carry-over of approval 'in principle' for a new project, which would draw upon this money. Given the extended difficulties over land purchase for the existing site, the management committee and centre workers considered the possibilities of developing on another site. This was a proposed capital development for a new-build Children's Centre to be located in the grounds of a grant-maintained primary school with which Sheffield Children's Centre had been working for several years. While the centre had not abandoned its plans for purchase of the land adjoining the centre, it was not by this time optimistic that this plan would secure the necessary income to proceed as it had been told that there would be no need for any additional services in the Sharrow area. It had also been informed that the hub and satellite model of service provision was being replaced with the extended schools agenda, and that new Children's Centres were to be aligned with existing schools. Flexible as ever, the centre looked to diversify in new ways, still seeking to meet community need but in a new area of the city and in conjunction with a local school with which it already had well-established links.

The centre had been developing and providing family support and wrap-around services for the primary school. In recognising its increasing marginalisation from the local authority in relation to the Sharrow area, and still with the intention of securing its present level of service within the city, albeit with part of it relocated, the centre undertook a feasibility study and consultation exercise in relation to the school and area need. It developed a business plan, and commissioned architectural drawings in compliance with requests from the local authority and the DfES Sure Start Unit. It hosted consultation meetings and visits from Sure Start Regional Officers and a London-based DfES representative, to describe the project and its intended location.

The above-mentioned email had concluded with an expectation that the grant would be spent in 2005/06, 'but we could discuss if that caused problems'; the centre seemed to have approval and continued flexibility from the DfES for this project. However, attempts to secure meetings between the local authority, the DfES and centre representatives in making progress were to prove difficult to co-ordinate. On 12 October 2005, the DfES representative asked the local authority if it would support this project in the context of continued roll-out of Children's Centres across the city. After many emails from the centre to try to progress the matter, an email of 16 March 2006 from a DfES representative showed that no answer had been forthcoming from the local authority. By 26 April, the DfES representative was attempting to set up a meeting of all parties, which subsequently happened in early June, also attended by PB and others working with the centre to develop their co-operative activities. The local authority said that it had not received the business plans and related documents for the project, although the centre was in receipt of an email (dated May) from a local authority representative, stating that it was 'a sound business plan' and requesting a marketing section, which was then supplied. At the time of writing, neither of these initiatives has made progress.

The vision of Sheffield Children's Centre has been recognised as a strong one; its services have been acknowledged as flexible and extensive; the difficulty, it seems, is that those outside the centre remain unable to see the extent of the portfolio, or perhaps they mistrust what they hear. During the EEC evaluation, one local authority respondent noted: 'some of the claims about the work the centre does are treated with scepticism, both quality and quantity are not always believed'. Yet it has been acknowledged in several reports that Sheffield Children's Centre had influenced national policy development. The centre, it seems, is something of a paradox, an enigma to some outsiders.

In 2006, and supported by the Sheffield Cooperative Development Group, the centre submitted a request for a sustainability grant of £100,000 from the local authority. A sum of £20,000 was awarded. The centre is continuing to provide early education, childcare and family support services on the same site. The staffing has inevitably reduced as the services have diminished with the loss of EEC income. The centre supplements its income by providing a contact service for the local authority. This is a well-established but highly challenging service that the local authority has chosen to outsource. The centre tendered for this work in competition. Local authorities are required to provide this service for one or both parents, siblings and extended family members where the courts have deemed they can have only supervised contact with their children/siblings. These can be highly charged interactions where disconnected families, and sometimes angry and highly anxious parents and others, are coming together under the supervision of centre workers. These meetings need careful management and planning, and can be highly draining for supporting workers as they seek to facilitate some quality time between parents (and others) and often equally anxious children. Long-standing centre workers are now highly experienced but still find these meetings to be very demanding aspects of their work. Regular reports are submitted and, at times, there are requirements for related court appearances. This work does generate essential income but workers have also always prioritised this work with some of the most vulnerable members of the community as a means of empowerment and inclusion.

The centre is also funded for a number of places for 3–4 year olds under the early education grant. But this presents it with some financial difficulties. An afternoon session would run from 1–6 pm and cost £22 per child. The grant pays £8.20 per child for a two-and-a-half-hour session. In the cases where the parents cannot afford to pay for the remainder of the session, the centre takes up the cost of the child remaining for the unpaid period. The centre has lost revenue from that place and this has continuing, incremental impact in relation to sustainability. If the centre were to ask the parent to remove the child after the funded period, this would have implications in relation to access and inclusion. This funding strategy of course is not a local authority decision but emerges from national policy.

In different ways, each of the previous chapters has illustrated how the centre has evolved over time, creating initiatives to meet participants' needs and preferences. The premises of diversity being the norm rather than the exception carry clear implications in that no service can foresee the best ways to deal with everybody's needs. It is necessary to listen to every participant's voice and reach agreements that, in so far as it is possible, satisfy every party. Each time an action is planned or evaluated it is necessary to reconstruct participants' notions, knowledge and experiences. We have illustrated how this means that, within the community, rules and ultimately identity are discussed and modified in order to remain inclusive and allow diversity to exist and flourish. This process, naturally, has not always worked and some members have left the heartland or decided not to join the network of support around the centre. The process, however, has not only supported innovation but, crucially, has made negotiation an essential part of the everyday activities of the centre. Because the origins of the centre were within a resistance to culturally inappropriate practices through participation, the core values of participants both resist and propose alternatives to outside practices, which seem to detrimentally affect its members. In this sense, innovation is valuable as long as it resists and opposes exclusion and marginalisation from decision-making. The project identity created alongside the development of the centre sees social justice and anti-discrimination predominantly around the notions of inclusion and involvement, and those derived and adapted to particular contexts. Innovation is part of the struggle for recognition.

It is likely that government representatives, and perhaps also community members, do not always share a vision on notions such as involvement, social justice, inclusion and democracy (Ross and Kemshall, 2000; Chinsinga, 2005), and that this mismatch can turn into an obstacle to programme implementation on occasion. Some examples of this have, we feel, been detailed above.

## Part 2: what can be learned from the story of Sheffield Children's Centre towards the future development of local services for children and families?

There are two tenets that rest at the heart of the provision made by Sheffield Children's Centre. These are, first, that the centre is built around and develops from a shared understanding that the only way to develop services for children and families that are socially just, culturally sensitive and inclusive is to build those services from the ground up in partnership with the adults, children and young people within the local community. These 'local projects' have emerged from the service users themselves, both adult and children, both young and old; they have emerged also from the workers in consultation with service users. The local projects emerge from sometimes challenging, but fundamentally trustful, dialogues between service users and service providers, whereby community members, particularly those experiencing difficulties, come to believe that their experiences and needs will be responded to in non-judgemental ways. Workers are forthcoming about their own personal difficulties and experiences in these conversations, and also draw on their own experiences to initiate and sustain service development. There is a perceived cultural consonance between service users and service providers that is both promoted by and reflected in the diversity within the staffing in relation to race, ethnicity, disability and gender, and this supports the growth of cultural consonance and sustains the dialogues because shared understandings become evident in the ongoing dialogues. The principles of local projects and a striving for social justice have also driven the work of the centre as it has developed international initiatives and links.

The second fundamental tenet that rests at the heart of its provision is in acknowledging and accepting that an inherent respect for diversity is never a given in any service provision; individuals must collectively strive to achieve it through constantly challenging their own stereotypical and partial views of the world and through personal education, attitude change and experiences beyond their own cultural backgrounds and identities. This is a never-ending process of personal and professional development, where service providers and service users together seek to recognise that all aspects of diversity are integral to community life. Chapter 4 spoke of diversity as 'a diamond with many facets'. A diamond needs to be cut and polished to shine, and time has to be devoted to each of those facets; collective action can arise only from a personal and continuing commitment to shared principles of practice – these grow, they cannot be imposed. This is not an issue for occasional consideration at the centre; it is a daily confrontation with possibility that manifests itself at all levels from family support services to the curriculum in action, from employment policy to equal opportunities policy, from the implementation of co-operative principles to the search for social justice across communities located locally, nationally and internationally.

This book has aimed to illustrate the vision in action at Sheffield Children's Centre, indeed to try to understand and articulate the vision. We saw in Chapter 1 that many of the workers were drawn to the centre because of its co-operative principles and practices; many of the unpaid workers stay for the same reasons. There is a sense of 'justice in action' that seems to pervade and with which some individuals seem to want to connect; this seems to be an integral part of the overall identity of the centre – its *heartland*, as we have referred to it before. As well as attracting unpaid workers, many of the workers find ways of associating with the centre through work that is paid elsewhere; they locate their work in the centre as a means of fulfilling their paid responsibilities and of contributing to a social ethic in which they believe. This is perhaps a further strand of the cultural consonance that we discussed above and connects with the discussions in Chapter 1 from Dahlberg and Moss's work (2005) around notions of 'the Other'. The centre becomes a place where people's lives find a deeper meaning, both through their work and, for service users, through overcoming their difficulties and then making a contribution in relation to others in difficulty. Work and self become a unified experience. Within this heartland, everyone has the potential to become a *catalyst for change*, if they wish, and they begin to recognise this as they see the day-to-day impact of their work and their personal experiences on the lives and aspirations of others in the community.

However, and most crucially, the vision is not static; neither is it owned by one person nor guided by a top-down policy initiative. In the way the centre works is illustrated that, in a responsive and respectful culture, the vision has to be a dynamic one, one that can be shaped and reshaped by individuals working collaboratively, in this case within a co-operative ethos. In contrast to this, we might also argue that bureaucratic processes dim the collective vision of urban movements with common interests by robbing them of flexibility and responsiveness in the hard-and-fast search for target achievement and proven value for money. In creating a project identity that prioritises community influences on social change and that foregrounds group identity, the workers and service users at Sheffield Children's Centre run the risk of existing outside the mainstream, even while creating structures, systems and policies that the mainstream professes it wishes to emulate.

Some argue (Foster and Meinhard, 2005; Gustafsson and Driver, 2005; Laforest and Orsini, 2005) that policy development based on target attainment disempowers non-governmental organisations and community-based initiatives because target-setting has taken place without listening to community members, who are integral participants within these types of services. The same thing happens when community members are excluded from decisions regarding programme implementation and evaluation (Driver and Martell, 2002). Policy-makers could argue that they need to make sure resources are best used with careful, associated planning, but it is necessary to consider how community involvement and ultimately democracy can actually be promoted within programmes such as EEC and the Sure Start Local Programme if these are to be more than discourse or empty rhetoric (Lister, 2000; Cook, 2002; Dorsner, 2004).

Individuals and families experience social exclusion for a wide range of reasons. In creating a heartland where social exclusion is confronted through daily activity and through collective pursuit of service development, the centre places reciprocity at the heart of the heartland as a pulse that drives the emerging project identity. From this reciprocity, and founded on co-operative principles, emerge flexibility and service expansion. New initiatives do not emerge in response to new targets but come from the ground up, presented by adults and children, and recognised by workers and leaders in the centre. One of the key aspects that underpins the continuation and development of the centre is something we can best describe as 'incremental reciprocity'. It has been stated above and elsewhere that this reciprocity is at the heart of the heartland. While reciprocity is nurtured by the collective intent of workers and service users (adults and children), this would be insufficient without strong leadership and, equally, without the commitment and motivation of the workers. The interconnectedness across these aspects is what generates and sustains this incremental reciprocity, and also what fuels the holistic and dynamic nature of the centre and its work, along with a healthy dose of humour and a shared history that is nurtured by retold stories of people, places, events, sadness and achievements. However, it would be wrong to say that this 'dynamic nature of the centre' is self-perpetuating; as a structure it is both powerful and vulnerable. It is powerful because it can bring about lasting benefits for children and families, as we have seen from the testimonies upon which this book has drawn. It is most fundamentally vulnerable because it is at the opposite end of a continuum to a mainstream approach that is inherently bureaucratic, hierarchical and target driven. In effect, Sheffield Children's Centre may be successful because it sits outside the mainstream and is driven by a different set of ethics, but it is also vulnerable for the same reasons.

The workers, both paid and unpaid, see themselves as having common ground and, often, shared experiences with service users. This is a strength of the service in that it positions workers alongside the community rather than as servicing the community from the position of 'experts'. The workers and service users see themselves as connecting with an underpinning ideology that drives the vision of the centre, and as adding to that vision through their collaborative actions and initiatives. This extends to young people and to children as service users, as well as to adults; young people recognise and welcome the equity within which they are engaged and respond with creativity and generosity as they come to understand the meaning of a society built upon social justice principles.

Many of those for whom the centre is most successful and on whom much of this book has focused are those who live with different levels of poverty and difficulty and who, for a wide range of reasons, are marginalised within society – although of course there are more prosperous service users at the centre too. The preceding chapters have chronicled the Labour government's initiatives aimed at reducing poverty, particularly among children, but we have also pointed out the government's intention, in line with global aspirations, to create and maintain a high degree of overall, economic supremacy. As Chapter 1 pointed out, the key challenge is to keep the lives of the poor and the oppressed in sight, simultaneously. This Labour government chose to do this through the Sure Start initiative, aiming to spend £2.2 billion on revenue and over £1 billion on capital for Children's Centres and Sure Start programmes over the four years from 2004–08 (National Audit Office, 2006) – and of course considerable sums were spent prior to this period. This audit also indicates the difficulties that the existing centres are experiencing in reaching families with high levels of need in their areas; only 9 of the 30 included in the audit could evidence some success in this respect. The report concluded that less progress was being made in improving services for fathers, parents of children with disabilities and for ethnic minorities in areas with smaller minority populations – all areas where we have evidenced success for Sheffield Children's Centre in the preceding pages.

Through its networks of relationships and resources, the Sheffield Children's Centre has been able to improve the lives of many of its participants. The centre has created a process that considers the people not the 'problem' and within which the people themselves are seen as part of the solution and not a reason for the problem. By thinking and acting co-operatively in this way, the centre creates forms of knowledge that mainstream services are, it seems, still struggling to construct and share. Arguably, these forms of knowledge can be constructed only from the 'ground up', generating a heuristic nature that allows a direct relationship between discovery of knowledge and relevance of service development. This knowledge cannot be transmitted through 'training' – it has to be generated and shared 'in situ'; it works best when it grows in context and when it is fed by opportunities for shared understandings among workers to grow, from their experiences and discussion. Experiences can be traumatic because any individual might still experience 'cultural dissonance' because of the behaviour of service users (or perhaps of fellow workers), these behaviours being outside the cultural experiences of some individuals, but this is reflected upon within a context of acceptance of diversity. Experts mentor newcomers not as 'trainers' but as equals within the community, aiming to broaden horizons and experiences.

Let us remind ourselves once again that in its earliest stages of development, and for a substantial period, the target attainment-driven evaluation of the Sure Start Local Programmes was framed around the enhanced recruitment of the 'hard to reach' to local services. This embedded this deficit construct in local initiative debate about and delivery of services, and subsequently drove it forward, in conceptually influential and deeply embedded ways, into the national Children's Centre programme. The construct of 'hard to reach' is diametrically opposite to the frames of reference that underpin the work with children and families at Sheffield Children's Centre. We have noted, above, the recent report on the developing Children's Centres, in a National Audit Office study (2006), which shows that over two-thirds of the centres covered by the audit are still failing to reach the neediest families. This aspect of expanded provision for children and families has proved to be among the most challenging within service development. There should be no assumptions made about any homogeneity among those who do not take up services. They are a diverse group and service providers must take account of this diversity (Barlow *et al.*, 2005). This National Audit Office study also suggests that non-professional volunteers or befrienders may be more effective at attracting non-service users, a model clearly evident at Sheffield Children's Centre. It has also been shown that retaining service users requires an ongoing and active engagement by service providers; supporting access is merely the first step, it is not a one-off task (Garbers *et al.*, 2006).

What has be seen in the preceding chapters of this book is that the alternative conceptualisation of service development from that of 'hard to reach' – a stigmatised and demeaning label – might be the working construct of 'word of mouth'; that trust grows and marginalised individuals and families approach a service because people they know and believe have said that they should, because those people know that they have found a social heartland, a project identity with which they can identify and within which they might flourish. They have experienced fluidity to service development, almost as a river finds its course. This is a direct contrast to target-driven development, which inevitably takes little account of community concerns and aspirations as a starting point for service development.

At the Sheffield Children's Centre is found a heartland that seeks to value experiences and lifestyle choices, and that recognises and accepts that not all families can control the influences on those experiences and choices all of the time. There is a sense of communal and cultural identity, but this is not monolithic and for all participants those identities shift and change as time and circumstances move forward. No one assumes that anyone – whether service provider or service user, whether adult or child – will remain the same with the passage of time. From this point of view, improving children's lives cannot be achieved without improving families and developing communities. This is possible, we would contend, only when all parties are able to establish and develop relevant relationships that allow them to share knowledge and experience aimed at improving common conditions.

During Marco Delgado's research at the centre, he had asked Jenny what kept her working at the centre and she replied:

I think it's just loyalty [laughs] and I think it probably goes for the sake of everybody. Of course you've got to be committed to this area of work. I think more and more it's about not letting people down and getting stuck in. Not walking away from the others. The situation now is that you can also really feel that you can make a difference. And I think we are getting more and more wound down by the process of external agencies' attack, but we will fight to the end. So I think it's standing your ground and letting them know we are here, also loyalty to the people of the community and the others and members of the management committee.

(Delgado, 2006: 247)

The work at Sheffield Children's Centre grew out of an ethic of resistance to cultural inappropriateness for vulnerable children and families; from this its project identity emerged and became influential, establishing that identity and its influence nationally and internationally. The resistance to a detrimental impact from outside influences continues to drive the will and the work of the centre and will undoubtedly do so for as long as they can function within the communities they support. We have sought in this book to shed light on the relationship between resistance and innovation in a local project. In the next section, we briefly consider some issues relating to the way policy development might respond to these inherent tensions between discourses and might, in doing so, begin to emphasise notions such as community involvement, democracy and innovative programme implementation.

So what are the implications from this in-depth study of Sheffield Children's Centre in relation to the continuing roll-out of Children's Centres in England, some of which are in new builds, some of which are attached to primary or secondary schools within the emerging Extended Services around School and Children's Centres agenda, and some of which have developed from existing services? They have arisen from an underpinning principle of service provision for those in disadvantaged communities, and yet there is no national policy relating to how those services will be sustainable for those unable to pay for them, other than the funding for 3 and 4 year olds for early education which, as we have seen above, can actually diminish the income of independent providers. (This is also being extended to 2 year olds in pilot projects around the country.)

As the Sure Start Local Programme funding disappears, and as local authorities make decisions on which services to fund and which to end (all of which will have been developed for the 'hard to reach'); they will inevitably and unavoidably be cutting services to those most in need. In local communities, those least inclined to access local services may once again be marginalised. If the new community services are in schools, we must ask ourselves how far these buildings and organisations can be successful in truly attracting those members of society, of whom there are many, who remain on the margins of, or outside, what is perceived as 'society' by those whose key agenda, in the present climate, inevitably relates to maintaining and improving standards rather than to the promotion of social justice. We might also ask – and this is perhaps the book's most important question – why government policy cannot be sufficiently creative and flexible to allow services for children and families that operate effectively and independently of a local authority to be directly funded. The spirit of enterprise and innovation is always more likely to come from the small, independent community provider, where flexibility and innovation are the key to service development and sustainability rather than from the lumbering bureaucracy, inevitably hidebound by its size and inflexibility.

We would say that the keys to the success and longevity of Sheffield Children's Centre are the respect for and understanding of diversity, equity, inclusion and anti-discriminatory practice that have evolved over time, within its ethos and culture; the centre polishes that diamond whenever it can, and through some difficult and demanding times, because it works from a first principle of respect for all. This principle now needs to find greater voice in mainstream services if Children's Centres are to become an entitlement for all rather than a service for those confident enough to come calling.

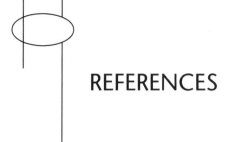

# REFERENCES

Armistead, J. (2004) Just starting out: researching young children's perspectives of early education and childcare and gaining informed consent from children. Paper presented at the British Educational Research Association, Early Years Special Interest Group, University of Warwick, May.

Armistead, J. (2005) Listening to the experts – three and four year olds' perspectives of nursery. Paper presented at British Educational Research Association Student Conference, University of Glamorgan, September.

Armistead, J. (2006) 'I wasn't allowed in the kitchen'; finding out how much children know about their day nursery. Paper presented at the European Early Childhood Education Research Association, Reykjavik, September.

Baker, J., Lynch, K., Cantillon, S. and Walsh, J. (2004) *Equality, From Theory to Action*. Hampshire: Palgrave Macmillan.

Baldock, P. (2001) *Regulating Early Years Services*. London: David Fulton Publishers.

Barlow, J., Kirkpatrick, S., Stewart-Brown, S. and Davies, H. (2005) Hard-to-reach or out-of-reach? Reasons why women refuse to take part in early interventions. *Children and Society* 19: 199–210.

Bertram, T., Pascal, C., Bokhari, S., Gasper, M. and Holtermann, S. (2001) *Early Excellence Centre Programme 2nd Annual Evaluation Report 2000–2001*. London: DfES (RR 361).

Blair, T. (1999) 'Beveridge re-visited: a welfare state for the 21st century', in R. Walker (ed.) *Ending Child Poverty. Popular Welfare for the 21st Century*. Bristol: Policy Press: 7–18.

Bourdieu, P. (1986) The forms of capital, in J.G. Richardson (ed.) *Handbook for Theory and Research for the Sociology of Education*. New York: Greenwood Press: 241–258.

Bradbury, G. and Jantti M. (1999) Child poverty across industrialised nations. *Innocenti Occasional Papers, Economic and Social Policy series no 71*. Florence: Unicef.

Bradley, M. (1982) *The Coordination of Services for Children under Five*. Berkshire: NFER-Nelson Publishing Company.

Brunsden, E. and May, M. (2002) Evaluating New Labour's approach to independent welfare provision, in M. Powell (ed.) *Evaluating New Labour's Welfare Reforms*. Bristol: Policy Press.

Burchinal, M.R. and Cryer, D. (2003) Diversity, child care quality and developmental outcomes. *Early Childhood Research Quarterly* 18 (4), Winter: 401–426.

Calhoun, C.I. (1994) Social theory and the politics of identity, in C.I. Calhoun (ed.) *Social Theory and the Politics of Identity*. Oxford: Blackwell Publishing.

Castells, M. (2000) *The Rise of the Network Society*. (2nd edn). Malden: Blackwell Publishing.

Castells, M. (2004) *The Power of Identity*. (2nd edn). Malden: Blackwell Publishing.

Chinsinga, B. (2005) The clash of voices: community-based targeting of safety net interventions in Malawi. *Social Policy and Administration* 39 (3): 284–301.

Clark, A. and Moss, P. (2001) *Listening to Young Children: The Mosaic Approach*. York: Joseph Rowntree Foundation London: National Children's Bureau.

Clemens, S., Ullman, A. and Kinnaird, R. (2005) *The 2005 Childcare and Early Years Providers Survey* (RR764). Nottingham: DfES.

Cohen, B. and Moss P. (2004) *A New Deal for Children? Re-forming Education and Care in England, Scotland and Sweden*. Bristol: Policy Press.

Cook, D. (2002) Consultation for change? Engaging users and communities in the policy process. *Social Policy and Administration* 36 (5): 516–531.

Co-operative Action (undated) *Co-operative Capital: A New Approach to Investment in Co-operatives*. Manchester: Co-operative Action.

Dahlberg, G. and Moss, P. (2005) *Ethics and Politics in Early Childhood Education*. London: RoutledgeFalmer.

Daniel, P. and Ivatts, J. (1998) *Children and Social Policy*. New York: Palgrave.

Delgado, M.A. (2006) Community involvement in services for young children, families and communities: accepting, resisting and opposing alternatives to mainstream views. Unpublished PhD thesis, University of York, Department of Educational Studies.

DfEE (1996) *Work and Family: Ideas and Options for Childcare. A Consultation Paper*. London: DfEE (distributed by Westex).

DfES (2003) *Every Child Matters: Change for Children. The Green Paper* (Cm 5860). London: The Stationery Office.

Dorsner, C. (2004) Social exclusion and participation in community development projects: evidence from Senegal. *Social Policy and Administration* 36 (1): 46–61.

Driver, S. and Martell, L. (2002) New Labour, work and the family. *Social Policy and Administration* 36 (1): 46–61.

Foster, M.K. and Meinhard, A.G. (2005) Diversifying revenue sources in Canada. Are women's voluntary organisations different? *Non-profit Management and Leadership* 16 (1): 43–60.

Franklin, A. (1999) Starting at the beginning: an early years approach to social inclusion – Sheffield, in K.J. White (ed.) *Children and Social Exclusion*. London: Unit 4 Open University Press.

Freire, P. (1970) *Education as the Practice of Freedom: Cultural Action for Freedom*. Cambridge: Harvard Educational Review/Center for the Study of Development.

Freire, P. (1972) *Pedagogy of the Oppressed*. Harmondsworth: Penguin Books.

Freire, P. (1973) *Education for Critical Consciousness*. New York: Seabury.

Freire, P. (1987) *A Pedagogy for Liberation: Dialogues on Transforming Education*. Basingstoke: Macmillan.

Freire, P. (1999) Education and community involvement, in M. Castells (ed.) *Critical Education in the New Information Age*. Lanham: Lowman & Littlefield: 37–64.

Garbers, C., Tunstill, J., Allnock, D. and Akhurst, S. (2006) Facilitating access to services for children and families: lessons from Sure Start Local Programmes. *Child and Family Social Work* 11: 287–296.

Giddens, A. (1998) *The Third Way*. London: Policy Press.

Gilchrist, A. (2004) *Community Cohesion and Community Development; Bridges or Barricades?* London: Community Development Foundation, in conjunction with the Runnymede Trust.

Gillies, V. (2005) Meeting parents' needs? Discourses of 'support' and 'inclusion' in family policy. *Critical Social Policy* 25 (1): 70–90.

Gregg, P., Harkness, S. and Machin, S. (1999) Poor kids: child poverty in Britain 1966–96. *Fiscal Studies* 20: 163–187.

Gustaffson, U. and Driver, S. (2005) Parents, power and public participation: Sure Start, an experiment in New Labour governance. *Social Policy and Administration* 39 (5): 528–543.

HMSO (1989) *The Children Act*. London: The Stationery Office.

[help]HM Treasury – This reference is missing[/help]

HM Treasury (2004) *Choice for Parents, the Best Start for Children*. London: The Stationery Office.

Howarth, C. and Kenway, P. (1998) *Monitoring Poverty and Social Inclusion: Why Britain Needs a Key Indicators Report*. York: Joseph Rowntree Foundation.

Kellmer, P. and Naidoo, S. (1975) *Early Childcare in Britain* (International Monograph Series on Early Childcare). New York: Columbia University Press.

Laforest, R. and Orsini, M. (2005) Evidence-based engagement in the voluntary sector: lessons from Canada. *Social Policy & Administration* 39 (5): 481–497.

Langsted, O. (1994) Looking at quality from the child's perspective, in P. Moss and A. Pence (eds) *Valuing Quality in Early Childhood Services*. London: Paul Chapman Publishing.

Levinas, E. (1987) *Time and the Other*. Pittsburgh, PA: Duquesne University Press.

Lister, R. (2000) Towards a citizens welfare state. The 3+2 Rs of welfare reform. *Theory Culture and Society* 18 (2–3): 91–111.

Mayall, B. (2000) Conversations with children: working with generational issues, in P. Christensen and A. James (eds) *Research with Children: Perspectives and Practices*. London: RoutledgeFalmer: 120–135.

Meleady, C. and Broadhead, P. (2002) The norm not the exception – putting diversity in its place in provision for children and families. *Children in Europe* 2: 14–16.

Millar, J. and Ridge, T. (2002) Parents, children, families and New Labour: developing family policy?, in M. Powell (ed.) *Evaluating New Labour's Welfare Reforms*. Bristol: Policy Press.

Morrissey, M. (2003) Briefing paper: a diagnostic tool for the analysis of community tension. Unpublished paper, University of Ulster.

Moscovici, S. (1976) *Social Influence and Social Change*. London: European Association of Experimental Social Psychology & Academic Press.

Moss, P. and Pence, A. (1994) (eds) *Valuing Quality in Early Childhood Services*. London: Paul Chapman Ltd.

Mugny, G. and Perez, J. (1987) *The Social Psychology of Minority Influence*. Cambridge: Cambridge University Press.

Myers, R. (1992) *The Twelve Who Survive. Strengthening Programmes of Early Childhood Development in the Third World*. London: Routledge, UNESCO and CGECCD.

National Audit Office (2006) *Sure Start Children's Centres*. London: HMSO.

*Nursery World* (2005) UK centre workers front aid effort, 27 October: 5.

Owen, C. (2003) Men in the nursery, in J. Brannen and P. Moss (eds) *Rethinking Children's Care*. Buckingham: Open University Press.

Prott, R. and Preissing, P. (eds) (undated) *Bridging Diversity – An Early Childhood Curriculum*. Berlin: Verlag das Netz, translated by Dr Ann Robertson.

Prout, A. (2003) Participation, policy and the changing conditions of childhood, in C. Hallett and A. Prout (eds) *Hearing the Voices of Children. Social Policy for a New Century*. London: RoutledgeFalmer.

Pugh, G. (1988) *Services for Children Under Five; Developing a Coordinated Approach*. London: National Children's Bureau.

Pugh, G. (1990) Developing a policy for early childhood education: challenges and constraints. *Early Child Development and Care* 58: 3–13.

Putnam, R. (1993) *Making Democracy Work*. New Jersey: Princeton University Press.

Rahman, M., Palmer, G., Kenway, P. and Howarth, C. (2000) *Monitoring Poverty and Social Exclusion*. York: Joseph Rowntree Foundation.

Reed, H. and Stanley, K. (2005) *Co-operative Social Enterprise and its Potential in Public Service Delivery*. Manchester: Co-operatives UK.

Ross, L. and Kemshall, H. (2000) Partners in evaluation: modelling quality in partnership projects. *Social Policy & Administration* 34 (5): 551–566.

Santos, B. de S. (1995) *Towards a New Common Sense: Law, Science and Politics in the Paradigmatic Transition*. London: Routledge.

Satterfield, T. (1996) Pawns, victims or heroes: the negation of stigma and the plight of Oregon's loggers. *Journal of Social Issues* 52 (1): 71–83.

Willis, P. (1999) Labour power, culture and the cultural commodity, in M. Castells (ed.) *Critical Education in the New Information Age*. Lanham: Rowman & Littlefield: 139–169.

Woodhead, M. and Faulkner, D. (2000) Subjects, objects or participants? Dilemmas of psychological research with children, in P. Christensen and A. James (eds) *Research with Children*. London: RoutledgeFalmer.

Woolcock, M. (2001) The place of social capital in understanding social and economic outcomes in Isuma. *Canadian Journal of Policy Research* 2 (1): 11–17.

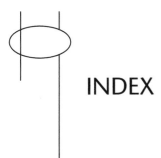

# INDEX